Middle Eastern Cooking
A Practical Guide

Middle Eastern Cooking
A Practical Guide

Samia Abdennour

Photographs by
Ola Seif

The American University in Cairo Press

To my beloved family
Samir, Soha, Reda, and Hana
Samer, Salma, and Souhail

Copyright © 1997 by
The American University in Cairo Press
113 Sharia Kasr el Aini
Cairo, Egypt

Second printing 1999

Dar el Kutub No. 7311/96
ISBN 977 424 401 X

Printed in Egypt

Contents

Introduction

The geographical location of the Middle East, mid-way between East and West (Asia and Europe), the conquests, travels, and trades, have all combined to allow it to draw on the riches of both cultures. The fertile agricultural valleys and the barren desert expanses have both left their marks on the lifestyle of the region.

For a very long time, a woman's role in the Middle East was restricted to the home—defined as her kingdom—to tend to the needs and pleasures of her family. The women of the family and neighborhood came together and devised intricate and elaborate recipes to delight the men. Customs die hard, and now with modern changes in Middle Eastern society, where women need to work outside as well as inside the home, they still prepare the same painstaking dishes, but individually, no longer in a joyful gathering. To most Middle Easterners, food is more than a necessity—it is a way of living, thinking, and behaving.

I have chosen and described in this book the most popular dishes relished in the Middle East and hope you will also enjoy preparing and savoring their delicious taste.

Bi-l-hana wi-l-shifa.

1

Mezze

1   Mezze (Egypt) and Mukabbalat (Lebanon and
    Syria) — Mezze

This is an assortment of small dishes, like hors d'oeu-
vres, served with drinks, as appetizers, or as side dishes.
Mezze comprises a large selection of dishes that can serve as
meals in themselves. Though many of these dishes, such as
stuffed vine leaves, fried liver, tabuli, etc. form part of the
mezze, yet they are mentioned only under their respective
entries.

In Iran, mezze consists mainly of a large bowl of different fresh herbs, depending on seasonal availability.

2   Aginares oma — Artichoke hearts
    Cyprus

6-8 artichoke hearts
2 tablespoons lemon juice
1 lemon, peeled and sliced
celery sticks

Cut artichoke hearts into quarters, place in a deep
bowl, and sprinkle with lemon juice. Add salted water to
barely cover and marinate for 1 hour.

Remove from marinating juice, pat dry, and serve with
celery sticks and slices of lemon.

3   Fuul nabit — Bean sprouts

Egypt, Lebanon, Syria, and Jordan

1/2 kg dried broad beans
2 large onions, quartered or sliced
10–15 garlic cloves, crushed
2–3 tablespoons lemon juice
1 teaspoon cumin powder
hot pepper (optional)
1 tablespoon parsley leaves, chopped
salt

Choose one of these two methods of preparation before actually cooking the beans:

a. Soak the beans in an earthenware or glass container for 4–6 days, rinsing and changing the water every 12 hours. The beans are ready when they have germinated at least 1 cm.

b. Soak the beans for 24 hours, then rinse, drain, and cover with a wet cloth. Repeat this procedure for 4–6 days, until the beans germinate about 2–3 cms.

The second of these methods (b) gives the beans a stronger, nutty flavor, since soaking the beans in water (a), makes them softer and therefore able to absorb more juice.

Place the germinated beans in a pot with onions, cover with water, and boil for 20–30 minutes or until beans are soft. Add garlic, lemon juice, cumin, salt, and hot pepper (if used) and boil for another 5–7 minutes.

To test if cooked, squeeze bean between thumb and forefinger. If the skin comes off easily, they are ready. Remove from flame and spoon into glass or earthenware container together with liquid. Allow to cool, then add chopped parsley and stir gently.

Eat germinating beans without their outside covering. Hold the bean between thumb and forefinger, bite on bean, press into mouth, and discard skin. If you like, serve the juice in small cups.

4   Tavuk jolesi — Jellied chicken
       Turkey

       2 small chickens (less than 1 kg each)
       1 carrot, peeled and diced
       1 onion, chopped very fine
       2 tablespoons celery, stalks and leaves chopped very
           fine
       2 tablespoons parsley, chopped very fine
       1 egg, with shell
       1 teaspoon lemon juice
       2 tablespoons almond slivers
       1 teaspoon gelatin

   Boil chicken with vegetables and lemon juice until
tender. Remove from pot, skin, bone, and cut chicken into
neat pieces. Place in deep bowl or cake mold. Drain stock,
discard vegetables, and return stock to flame. Break egg,
beat, crush shell with fingers, and toss entire egg into pot
with its shell crushed. Simmer gently for 10–15 minutes.
Strain and set aside, keeping warm.
   Dissolve gelatin in 1 tablespoon of water, stirring vig-
orously, then add to warm stock and pour over chicken
pieces. Chill, then turn over onto serving dish.

5   Hummus bi-l-tahina — Chickpeas with tahina sauce
       Lebanon, Syria, and Jordan

       1 cup chickpeas*
       1 cup tahina sauce, 156 or 157
       1 tablespoon lemon juice
       decoration
           parsley finely chopped
           chili powder
           oil
           slices of lemon

Soak chickpeas overnight. Drain, add fresh water, and simmer until tender (about 30 minutes). Drain, set aside a spoonful of whole chickpeas for decoration, and mash, pound, or pass the rest through a food processor. Add tahina sauce, lemon juice (though tahina is already acidulated, chickpeas taste better with more lemon juice), and blend until smooth. Sprinkle top with olive oil, and decorate with whole chickpeas, parsley, chili powder, and lemon slices.

* This bushy leguminous plant is also present in many other Mediterranean countries. It bears rounded pealike seeds; its Latin name is "cicer." It is said that Cicero was so nicknamed because of the pea-shaped wart on the end of his nose.

6   Murshan — Chickpeas and chard
     Tunisia

1 cup chickpeas
1 cup chard leaves, chopped coarsely
3–5 garlic cloves, crushed
1 onion, chopped very fine
1 tablespoon tomato paste
1 teaspoon coriander powder
red chili

Soak chickpeas overnight, drain, and boil until tender (do not discard boiling liquid).

Parboil chard for a few minutes, drain, and squeeze out moisture.

Blend coriander, red chili, and garlic to form a smooth paste.

Fry onion until just golden, add garlic mixture and tomato paste, and cook for 3–5 minutes, stirring continuously. Add chard, chickpeas, and enough of the boiled liquid to cover. Cook for another 10–15 minutes, stirring until it is all well blended.

7   Babaghanuuj — Roasted and puréed eggplant
         Lebanon, Syria, and Jordan

    1 kg brown round eggplant
    1 tablespoon lemon juice
    1 cup thin tahina sauce, 156 or 157
    1 tablespoon parsley, finely chopped
    1 tablespoon olive oil

Roast eggplant for 90–120 minutes, or until tender. (see 66). Mash and mix with tahina sauce and chopped parsley and sprinkle top with oil.

8   Bitinjan bi 'asir rumman — Roasted and puréed
         eggplant with pomegranate juice
         Lebanon

    1 kg brown round eggplant
    2 tablespoons pomegranate juice
    1 tablespoon pomegranate seeds
    olive oil, salt

Roast eggplant for 90–120 minutes, or until tender (see 66). Mash and mix with pomegranate juice and salt. Sprinkle top with oil and decorate with pomegranate seeds.

9   Bitinjan bi-l-laban — Roasted eggplant with yoghurt
         Lebanon

    1 kg brown round eggplant
    5–7 garlic cloves, crushed
    1 cup yoghurt
    1 teaspoon mint powder
    salt

Roast eggplant for 90–120 minutes, or until tender (see 66). Mash. Mix garlic with yoghurt and stir into eggplant. Sprinkle top with dried mint.

10   Melitzanosalata — Eggplant dip
        Cyprus

        1 kg round brown eggplant
        a chunk of stale bread
        3–5 garlic cloves, crushed
        2 tablespoons lemon juice
        1 tablespoon olive oil
        1 onion, grated
        2 tablespoons parsley, chopped very fine
        salt

        Roast eggplant for 90–120 minutes, or until tender
(see 66). Mash.
        Sprinkle bread with cold water, squeeze dry, crumble,
and add to eggplant with garlic, lemon juice, parsley, onion,
and salt, and mix thoroughly. Sprinkle with olive oil and
chill before serving.

11   Aqras kibbeh — Kibbeh patties
        Lebanon

        kibbeh, 111
        cooking oil

        Roll out kibbeh thinly (about 1/2 cms) on greased
surface. Cut into round discs about 5 cms in diameter and
fry until brown. Drain and serve warm or cold.

12   Kibda nayya — Raw liver*
        Palestine

        liver
        onions
        lemon juice
        fresh mint leaves
        salt and pepper

Rinse liver well and dice. Grate onions, mix with lemon juice, salt, and pepper and soak liver in this mixture for 1–2 hours. Brush off marinating juice and serve on a bed of fresh mint leaves.

* For this recipe, it is very important that the liver be fresh. Raw liver is usually enjoyed at Easter (for Christians) and at 'Id al-Adha (for Muslims), when the sacrificial lamb or calf is traditionally slaughtered at home.

13   Tirmis — Lupine
Egypt, Syria, Lebanon, and Jordan

1 cup lupine
salt

Soak lupine overnight, drain, add fresh water, and simmer over medium heat for 7–10 minutes, skimming whenever necessary. Drain, rinse with tap water, and soak again for 2–3 days, changing the water every 12 hours. By this time, the lupine should have lost its bitter taste. Soak again for 24–36 hours with 1 tablespoon of salt, repeating every 12 hours. Drain and serve.

The seeds are eaten without their outside covering. Hold seed between thumb and finger, bite on lupine, press into mouth and discard skin.

In many parts of the Middle East in summertime and at dusk, hand-drawn carts bearing mounds of these yellow seeds can frequently be seen on street corners. At irregular intervals, the vendor will sprinkle the seeds with fresh water from an *ulla* to prevent them from getting dry, while enumerating their merits in a cheerful singsong.

14   Mana'ish — Pastry with oregano spread
Palestine

dough
    1 kg best-quality flour
    1 tablespoon active dried yeast

1 teaspoon salt

1/2 teaspoon sugar

spread

1/2 cup ready-made thyme *(za'tar)* or, if unavailable, a mixture of:

3 tablespoons oregano

1 tablespoon sumac powder

1/2 teaspoon sesame seeds

1 cup olive oil

salt

Cream yeast and sugar in warm water and leave covered to bubble in warm place. Sift flour and salt, and add yeast and enough warm water to produce soft dough. Knead well until the dough is smooth and leaves the bowl clean. Let stand in a warm place for 2–3 hours, allowing the dough to rise to about double its original size. Lightly flour rolling pin and pastry board, and spread into rounds or squares 5–7 cms across. Let stand for 1 hour.

With your fingertips, make two or three dents in pastry and spread the za'tar or oregano mixture, allowing a small margin of dough all round. Bake in preheated hot oven until pastry is crisp and crusty, about 20 minutes.

This recipe was originally eaten at breakfast whenever families kneaded and baked their own bread at home, about every three or four days. Now that this custom is no longer practiced, mana'ish are enjoyed as appetizers.

15   Filfil rumi ma'li — Sweet green peppers, fried
     Egypt

1/2 kg green peppers

1 tablespoon vinegar

7–10 garlic cloves, crushed

cooking oil

salt

Slit the sides of the peppers, rub with salt, rinse, and pat dry. Heat oil and fry peppers until light brown. Remove onto absorbent paper and, when cool, discard stems and seeds and arrange neatly in serving dish.

Using the same oil, fry the garlic until golden, stirring constantly to prevent it from sticking to bottom of pan. Stir in vinegar and allow to bubble for 1–2 minutes before pouring over the peppers. Chill before serving.

16   Felfel moqli — Sweet green peppers, fried
      Tunisia

1/2 kg peppers
2 tablespoons vinegar
3–5 garlic cloves, crushed
olive oil
salt

Wash and dry peppers. Using a small knife, puncture each pepper near the stem and slip a pinch of salt into the hole. Let stand for 30 minutes. The salt extracts moisture from the peppers, which encourages steam to form and thus inhibits the oil from entering the incisions.

Heat olive oil and fry half the peppers, turning often until only lightly browned on all sides. Transfer to serving dish, setting aside some of the frying oil in a separate bowl for the dressing. Return pan to flame and fry the remaining peppers until well browned, them add them to the first batch, discarding the oil.

To make the dressing, mix vinegar, sugar, and garlic with the olive oil (already used and set aside), pour over the peppers, and stir until the peppers are well coated. Chill for 2–3 hours before serving.

17   Gibna 'arish — Skimmed cheese
      Egypt

This is a type of salt-free cheese that can be eaten by itself (it is very low in calories), but it is most often mashed coarsely with a fork or whirled in a slow electric mixer with any of the following mixtures of ingredients:

- a. Peeled and diced tomatoes, grated onion, finely sliced sweet peppers, salt, and pepper.
- b. Grated onion, crushed garlic, lemon juice, a few drops of oil, salt, and pepper.
- c. Chopped, pickled turnips and/or pickled eggplants and a few drops of oil.
- d. Grated onion, dash of mustard powder, chopped parsley leaves, salt, and pepper.
- e. Grated onion, crushed garlic, boiled beetroot, salt, and pepper.

Eat cheese with any of these mixtures by scooping it with morsels of local bread. If consistency is smooth and thin, these cheese mixtures can also be used as dip.

18   Bitingan mikhallil — Pickled eggplant
      Egypt

1 kg long brown eggplant
10–15 garlic cloves, crushed
1 teaspoon cumin powder
3 tablespoons vinegar
2 tablespoons parsley, chopped very fine
hot pepper (optional)
salt

Choose eggplants 10–12 cms long and 2–3 cms thick. Wash, tear away stem (do not use a knife), cover with water, and boil until tender. Drain, but do not discard liquid. Add salt and 1 tablespoon vinegar and allow to cool.

Mix garlic, cumin, hot pepper (if used), and parsley and wet with remaining vinegar. With a sharp knife, make a slit lengthwise in each eggplant, leaving 1 cm at each end. Without removing the pulp, spoon a small amount of the garlic mixture into each eggplant and arrange tidily in serving bowl. Pour in enough of the cooled liquid to cover the eggplants and serve.

19   Bitinjan makdus — Pickled eggplant
      Lebanon and Syria

      1 kg long brown eggplant
      10 garlic cloves, crushed
      1 cup walnuts, crushed
      hot pepper (optional)
      olive oil
      salt

Choose small eggplants 7–10 cms long and 1–2 cms thick. Parboil, rinse under tap water, pat dry, and set aside.

Mix garlic, walnuts, salt, and hot pepper (if used) and wet with olive oil. With sharp knife, make a slit lengthwise in each eggplant, leaving about 1 cm at each end. Spoon a small amount of the walnut mixture into each eggplant and arrange tidily in a glass jar. Cover with olive oil and seal tightly, shaking the jar gently every few days. The eggplants will be ready after about a week and will preserve well for a long time in oil.

20   Tamatim mikhallila — Pickled tomatoes
      Egypt

      8–10 small tomatoes
      5–7 garlic cloves, crushed
      1/2 teaspoon cumin

1 tablespoon vinegar

salt

Moisten the garlic, cumin, and salt with vinegar.
Serve in either of these two ways:

a. Slice the tomatoes, dip in garlic mixture, and arrange tidily in serving dish, sprinkling the rest of the mixture, if any, over the tomatoes

b. Make vertical cross-incisions in the tomatoes, being careful to leave their bases intact. Spoon some of the mixture into each tomato and arrange tidily in serving dish.

21   Khiyar mikhallil — Pickled cucumbers
Egypt

2 kgs cucumbers

6 cups water

3 tablespoons kitchen salt

2 tablespoons vinegar

20 garlic cloves, halved diagonally

1 cup celery, leaves and stalks chopped fine

hot pepper (optional)

Choose small thin cucumbers, 7–10 cms long and 2–3 cms in diameter.

Boil water and salt and place in pickling jar to cool. When tepid, stir in vinegar and add all the ingredients, alternating layers of cucumber, celery, and garlic, making sure to top with celery. If using peppers, chop with celery or halve and add to jar. Weigh down and cover tightly. The pickles should be ready in 24–36 hours.

22   Lamun mikhallil — Pickled limes
Egypt

50 limes, yellow, with smooth, spotless rinds

50 limes, to be squeezed for juice

4 tablespoons kitchen salt

3 tablespoons corncockle or black cumin

7 tablespoons safflower

Squeeze the juice of 50 limes. Mix safflower, corncockle, and salt.

Wash and dry the limes with the smooth rinds, then make vertical cross-incisions on them, being careful to leave bases attached. Fill with above mixture and arrange neatly in pickling jar, pressing down every layer and sprinkling with some mixture. When all the limes have been filled and placed in jar, cover with the rest of spice mixturè, if any. Pour the lime juice over the whole, weigh down, and cover tightly. Shake jar gently every few days. The pickled limes should be ready in 3–4 weeks.

Breakfast

23 Fuul midammis — Stewed broad beans
Egypt

2 cups dry broad beans
1/2 cup split lentils
1 each: tomato, carrot, and onion (optional)
oil
cumin
lemon juice
salt

Boil beans and lentils over quick flame with at least three times their measure in tap water, then add any or all of the optional vegetables. Cover very tightly and allow to simmer over very slow flame for 6–9 hours, or overnight, adding more boiling water (cold or tap water will shrivel the beans, change the taste, and make them hard) whenever the water level goes down and beans are not completely submerged.

This is the basis of fuul midammis. Add oil, lemon juice, salt, and cumin to this basic recipe. Crushed garlic, grated onions, chopped tomatoes, and pickles are also sometimes added.

A quicker but less attractive way to cook fuul midammis is to use a pressure cooker. Though the taste of

15

pressure-cooked beans remains mostly the same, they tend to turn much darker and taste more nutty; they therefore will need more of the additional ingredients.

24   Ta'miya (Egypt), Falafel (Jordan, Lebanon, and Syria) — Bean cakes

    2 cups skinned white broad beans*
    1/2 cup each: dill, coriander, and parsley leaves
    2 onions
    5–7 garlic cloves
    1 leek, stalk only
    1 teaspoon sodium bicarbonate or baking soda
    1 teaspoon cumin
    1/2 teaspoon cayenne pepper (optional)
    1–2 tablespoons sesame seeds
    cooking oil
    salt

Soak beans overnight. Drain and, using fine screen, mince with dill, coriander, onions, garlic, parsley, and leek. Add spices, seasoning, sodium bicarbonate, or baking soda and mix thoroughly (preferably with an electric mixer). Allow to stand for 1 hour at room temperature before frying.

With a wet spoon or wet fingers, scoop up a small amount, shape into flat rounds about 5 cms in diameter and 2 cms thick, sprinkle one side with sesame seeds, and deep fry in sizzling oil until brown. Remove onto absorbent paper and serve hot.

* This type of bean is called *fuul madshush*.

25   Labaneh — Yoghurt cheese
Lebanon, Jordan and Syria

    4 cups yoghurt
    1 tablespoon salt

olive oil

cheesecloth bag

Stir the salt into the yoghurt, rinse bag, pour the yoghurt into the bag, and tie up the opening. Hang the bag for 24 hours. Place a jug under it to collect the whey, which can be used in cooking or for drinking—it has great nutritive value. Remove labaneh from the bag, stir again, place in a glass jar, and sprinkle on top with olive oil.

Normally labaneh is made with goat's milk, which gives it a pleasant sour taste, but any other kind of milk will work just as well.

26   Fatut bi-l-hulba — Fried eggs with fenugreek
      Yemen

4–6 eggs

2 loaves local bread

1/2 cup ghee

1 tablespoon fenugreek, ground

1 tablespoon tomato paste

1/2 teaspoon zhug, 211

2 tablespoons lemon juice

2 cups chicken stock

salt and pepper

Prepare paste by blending fenugreek, tomato paste and zhug.

Break bread into bite-size morsels, heat ghee, and fry until crisp. Slide eggs onto pan and stir. Cook until scrambled eggs are well set.

Boil chicken stock with fenugreek paste on high heat uncovered until reduced to half its original volume, then add scrambled eggs and cook for another 3–5 minutes. Serve, adding lemon juice to each plate.

27   Beed maqli ma' jibneh — Fried eggs with white
      cheese
      Palestine

4–6 eggs
4–6 slices hard white cheese
olive oil
salt and pepper

Slice cheese 1 cm thick. Heat oil and fry, turning on
both sides to get the outside crisp. Remove and keep warm.
Fry eggs in the same oil, basting once or twice to firm up the
top. Season and serve beside the fried cheese.

28   Beed maqli ma' toom — Fried eggs with garlic
      Palestine

4–6 eggs
5–7 cloves garlic, crushed
1 tablespoon lemon juice
mint powder
olive oil
salt and pepper

Mix garlic with lemon juice, heat oil, and fry, stirring
constantly to prevent garlic from sticking to the bottom of
the pan. Slide eggs into pan, basting once or twice. When
set, sprinkle with mint powder and seasoning and serve.

29   Beed miza'lil (Egypt), beed mutajjan (Tunisia) —
      Fried hard-boiled eggs

4–6 hard-boiled eggs
1/2 teaspoon cumin powder
oil
parsley
salt and pepper

Shell the hard-boiled eggs, leaving them intact. Fry in sizzling oil, gently shaking the pan so that the eggs roll in the oil and brown all over. Remove from flame and place in serving dish, lined with parsley leaves. Mix cumin with seasoning and sprinkle on eggs.

30 Ispanakli yumurta — Fried eggs with spinach
Turkey

4–6 eggs
1/2 kg spinach
1 onion, chopped very fine
chunk of *beyaz peynir* (feta cheese), crumbled
cooking oil
salt and pepper

Rinse spinach in several changes of water, place in colander to drain, then shred coarsely.

Heat oil and fry onion until it wilts. Add shredded spinach and stir over medium heat until leaves wilt and liquid runs. Increase heat to cook spinach and reduce liquid, enough to cover base of pan only. Stir in crumbled cheese and seasoning and stir. Break eggs onto wilted spinach, spacing them evenly, then cover pan and cook over medium heat until eggs are set.

31 Cilber — Poached eggs
Turkey

4–6 eggs
1 cup yoghurt
3–5 cloves garlic, crushed
1 teaspoon vinegar
butter
dash of hot paprika
salt and pepper

Place yoghurt in moderately hot oven with garlic and seasoning. Poach eggs in water and vinegar. When set, add to yoghurt. In the meantime, melt butter and stir in the paprika, then dribble this pink butter over the eggs. Allow 2–3 minutes in the oven, put on individual plates, and season to taste.

32   Beed bi-l-laban — Baked eggs in yoghurt
Lebanon

> 4–6 eggs
> 1 egg white
> 2 cups yoghurt
> 5–7 cloves garlic, crushed
> 1 teaspoon mint powder
> ghee
> salt and pepper

Beat egg whites stiff, stir into the yoghurt, and place over very low flame to cook for 5–7 minutes. Pour into shallow oven dish and set aside.

Heat ghee in frying pan and fry garlic until golden—stirring constantly to keep it from sticking to the bottom of the pan. Add mint and stir.

Break eggs over yoghurt, spacing them evenly, pour the garlic and ghee mixture on top, and bake in oven until eggs are set.

33   'Igga baladi — Omelet (1)
Egypt

> 4–6 eggs
> 1 tablespoon flour
> 1 onion, chopped very fine
> dash of cinnamon powder
> cooking oil
> salt and pepper

Beat eggs, add sifted flour, cinnamon, and seasoning, and beat again. Heat oil and fry onion until golden, then stir in beaten eggs and fry on quick flame. When the underside sets, lift the edge or tilt the pan to let the liquid run underneath. Turn over and continue frying until both sides are golden and dry.

Omelets are usually served in thick slices.

34   `Igga baladi — Omelet (2)
      Egypt

      4–6 eggs
      1 tablespoon flour
      1 tablespoon parsley, chopped very fine
      dash of cumin
      cooking oil
      salt and pepper

Same as 33, but substitute parsley for onion and cumin for cinnamon.

35   Ojja bi-mergaz — Omelet with vegetables and
      sausages
      Tunisia

      4–6 eggs
      2 potatoes, peeled and diced very small
      2 tablespoons tomato paste
      5–7 cloves garlic
      5–7 spiced sausages, chopped very small
      1 teaspoon harissa, 214
      1 teaspoon paprika
      1 teaspoon caraway
      olive oil
      salt and pepper

Crush garlic with salt, paprika, and caraway seeds.

Heat oil and sauté potatoes then add tomato paste, garlic mixture, harissa, and enough water to just cover. Cook over low heat for 15 minutes. Add sausages and cook for another 15 minutes.

Beat eggs, pour over mixture, stir and serve immediately when eggs are set.

36   Ijjit nukha'aat — Brain omelet
      Lebanon, Syria and Jordan

    6 eggs
    1 sheep's brain
    1 onion, grated
    3 garlic cloves, crushed
    1 tablespoon lemon juice
    2 tablespoons parsley leaves, chopped very fine
    ghee
    salt and pepper

Cover brain in salted water and parboil. Drain, remove veins, and mash.

Heat ghee and lightly fry onion until it wilts, then add garlic and fry until golden, stirring constantly. Remove from flame.

Beat eggs and stir in all ingredients. Reheat ghee in a saucepan and fry egg mixture. When the underside sets, lift the edge to let the eggs run underneath. Turn over and continue to fry till both sides are golden and set. Slice into thick chunks and serve.

37   Kukuye bademjan — Eggplant omelet
      Iran

    6 eggs
    2 round brown eggplants
    1 onion, grated
    1/2 teaspoon cumin

1–2 cups yoghurt

ghee

salt and pepper

Peel and dice eggplant, sprinkle with salt, and allow to rest for 1 hour. Squeeze dry and fry until golden. Remove from flame and mash in deep bowl. Break eggs and add with onion, cumin, and seasoning to mashed eggplants, beating until smooth.

Reheat ghee and fry eggplant mixture. When the underside sets, lift edge to let eggs run underneath. Turn over and continue to fry till both sides brown. Slice into thick chunks and serve, covering each plate with yoghurt.

38   Kukuye sibzamini — Potato omelet or patties
        Iran

6 eggs

1/2 kg potatoes

1 onion, grated

1 teaspoon turmeric

ghee

salt and pepper

Peel and boil potatoes, place in a deep bowl, then mash. Break eggs and mix with all ingredients—except ghee—until smooth.

Heat ghee and fry the egg–potato mixture. When the underside sets, lift edge to let eggs run underneath. Turn over and continue to fry until both sides brown. Slice into thick chunks and serve. Or, to make patties, spoon out potato mixture, flatten to shape into patties, and deep fry in sizzling ghee. Remove onto absorbent paper and serve.

39   Sha'riya — Vermicelli
        Egypt

2 cups vermicelli

4 cups hot water

1 cup sugar

2 tablespoons raisins (optional)

milk

cooking oil

If the vermicelli comes in long filaments shaped into rounds, crush into pieces 2–3 cms long.

Heat oil and lightly fry raisins until they puff. Remove immediately and fry vermicelli until pale brown. Dissolve sugar in hot water and add to vermicelli together with raisins and cook over slow flame for 5–7 minutes. If vermicelli is not tender when the water is completely absorbed, sprinkle with more hot water. Serve, covering every plate with warm milk

For a richer dish, add chopped bananas, strawberries, and/or crushed mixed nuts to individual plates.

Main Courses

Artichokes

40   Artichokes

Clean raw artichokes, rinse under running tap or in several changes of water, and drain upside down. This will remove the grit and insects hidden between the leaves.

To prepare them for stuffing, remove the outside leaves from the artichokes then clip the remaining tips until they are neatly squared off. Gather the center leaves between thumb, index, and middle finger and gently twist and pull to remove the innermost leaves whole. Scrape the choke (the purple thorny part) so that the artichokes look like a cup. Soak in cold water and vinegar until ready for use.

41   Kharshuf mahshi — Stuffed artichokes
      Egypt

    12–14 artichoke hearts

    3–4 carrots

    1–2 onions

    2–3 cups meat stock

    1–2 tablespoons lemon juice

    stuffing

        savory minced beef, 100

Fill artichoke hearts with savory minced beef. Slice onions, carrots, and artichoke stalks. Mix all these vegetables and use them to line the bottom of the cooking pot. Arrange the artichoke hearts on top, cover with well-seasoned stock and cook over moderate flame. When ready, sprinkle with lemon juice and turn off flame. To serve, place cooked vegetables in the middle of the serving dish and surround with stuffed artichoke hearts.

42   Ard al-shoki mahshi — Stuffed artichokes
      Palestine

12–15 artichoke hearts
1/2 kg lamb, ground
2 onions, chopped very fine
1–2 tablespoons pine nuts
1 teaspoon cinnamon powder
fat (preferably lamb's tail)
salt and pepper

Heat fat and fry artichoke hearts. Remove onto absorbent paper. In the same fat, fry ground meat with onions until juice has been reabsorbed. Remove from flame, add seasoning and pine nuts, and mix well. Fill artichoke hearts with meat mixture, arrange tidily in pot, half cover with salted water, and cook over moderate flame.

43   Gannariya mihshiya — Stuffed artichokes
      Tunisia

12-15 artichoke hearts
1/2 kg lean beef, ground
2 tablespoons tomato paste
5 garlic cloves, crushed
1 onion, chopped very fine
2 tablespoons parsley, chopped very fine

2 tablespoons lemon juice

1 teaspoon tabil, 213

2 eggs

1 potato

cooking fat

dash of paprika

salt and pepper

Heat fat and fry half the crushed garlic, stirring constantly to keep it from sticking to the bottom of the pan, then stir in the tomato paste and seasoning, diluted in two cups of water. Allow to simmer for 5 minutes.

Place ground beef in pot with a half cup of water over high heat, stirring constantly. When water has evaporated, add onion and cook until onion wilts. Add parsley, remaining garlic, tabil, and seasoning and cook for 3 minutes longer. Set aside to cool.

Boil potato, drain, and mash. Beat eggs and add to meat with potatoes. Mix very thoroughly.

Fill artichoke hearts with this mixture, arrange tidily in pot, cover with tomato sauce, and cook until tender.

44   Ard al-shoki matbukh — Stewed artichokes
Palestine

10 artichoke hearts, quartered

1/2 kg peas, boiled

1/2 kg beef

2 onions, chopped

cooking fat

salt and pepper

Cut meat into bite-size cubes. Heat cooking oil and fry onions lightly, then add meat and fry. When juice has been reabsorbed, add enough water to barely cover, season, and cook.

When meat is nearly tender, add peas and artichoke hearts and cook for 10-15 minutes, adjusting seasoning and adding more hot water if there isn't enough liquid.

Beans

45   Bisara — Crushed beans with greens
      Egypt

> 1/4 kg crushed dried beans*
> 3 onions
> 10–15 garlic cloves
> 1 cup dill
> 1 cup parsley leaves
> 1 cup coriander leaves
> 1 teaspoon cumin powder
> 1 tablespoon mint powder
> 2 tablespoons oil
> 1 tablespoon dry mulukhiya,** crushed very fine
>   (optional)
> hot chili (optional)
> salt

Place crushed beans, garlic, dill, parsley, coriander, and 2 onions in a pot with plenty of water and boil until well cooked, about 60–90 minutes. Press in juice extractor or whirl in blender with enough of its liquid to get a custard-like consistency, then pass through a fine sieve. Return to flame, add cumin, mint, salt, and optional ingredients, and cook for a further 7–10 minutes.

In the meantime, slice the remaining onion very thinly and fry until nicely brown. Remove onions, strain the oil into the bisara, stir, then pour into shallow serving dish to cool. Decorate with the fried onions.

* This is called *fuul madshush*.

** A very popular Middle Eastern and African plant. Only the leaves are edible.

46   Fasulye plakisi — White bean stew
        Turkey

    2 cups dried haricot beans
    2 onions, chopped
    2 garlic cloves, crushed
    2 carrots, diced
    1 cup celery, stalk and leaves sliced very fine
    1/2 cup parsley, chopped very fine
    2 tablespoons tomato paste
    1 tablespoon lemon juice
    1/2 teaspoon sugar
    olive oil
    dash of chili
    salt and pepper

Soak beans for at least 2 hours. Drain, add fresh tap water, and boil in plenty of water for 3–5 minutes. Remove from flame and allow to rest for 1–2 hours.

Heat oil and fry onions until they wilt, then add garlic, carrots, and celery and fry for 3–5 minutes, stirring constantly.

Return beans to pot and boil for 30 minutes more. Dilute tomato paste in water, add sugar and seasoning, and toss into pot together with fried vegetables. Cook until tender.

Remove from flame, add lemon juice and parsley, adjust seasoning, and serve either hot or cold.

Cabbage

47 Cabbage

Choose firm cabbage with large, unruffled leaves. With the tip of a sharp knife, cut off each leaf separately, near the stem, and unfold gently. Cut out the middle hard part of leaves (do not discard; use to line the bottom of the pot). Boil water with salt and cumin and blanch leaves two or three at a time for about 2 minutes, or until they wilt. Remove with flat, perforated spoon and pile on sieve to drain.

To stuff, cut leaves to a size slightly larger than the palm of your hand. Place on a smooth surface and arrange stuffing on the thick end of leaf, across midrib, leaving about 1 cm on each side. The stuffing must be pencil-shaped. Fold in the sides to cover the stuffing, then roll the middle part.

48 Krumb mahshi — Stuffed cabbage
Egypt

1 cabbage
1/2 cup oil
2 tablespoons lemon juice
stuffing
    2 cups rice
    2 onions, grated
    3-4 tomatoes, peeled and diced
    1/2 cup parsley, chopped very fine
    1/2 cup dill, chopped very fine
    1/2 cup oil
    salt and pepper

Prepare cabbage leaves as in 47. Mix all stuffing ingredients together and fill cabbage leaves.

Line the bottom of the pot with the hard parts of leaves removed earlier, sprinkle 1 tablespoon of oil on top, then arrange stuffed cabbages on top. Cover with salted water. Sprinkle remaining oil on top, weigh down, and simmer over low flame for about 30 minutes. When cooked, turn over onto serving dish and discard the hard parts that lined the bottom of the pot. Sprinkle with lemon juice.

49   Dolmleh kalam — Stuffed cabbage
Iran

> 1 cabbage
> 2 tablespoons brown sugar
> 2 tablespoons vinegar (cider vinegar preferable)
> salt
> stuffing
>> 1/2 kg lamb or beef, ground
>> 1 onions, chopped very fine
>> 1 cup rice
>> 1 cup parsley, chopped very fine
>> 1/2 cup coriander, chopped very fine
>> 1 teaspoon turmeric

Prepare cabbage as in 47. Mix stuffing ingredients, fill cabbage leaves, and arrange neatly in cooking pot. Dilute sugar, vinegar, and salt in enough tap water to cover cabbages, then cook. When ready, turn over onto serving dish, and discard the hard parts that lined the bottom of the pot.

50   Malfuf mihshi bi-zayt — Stuffed cabbage, meatless
Lebanon

> 1 cabbage
> 1 teaspoon mint powder
> 5–7 garlic cloves, crushed
> 2 tablespoons lemon juice
> stuffing
>> 2 onions, chopped very fine
>> 2 tablespoons olive oil

1 cup rice

1 cup chickpeas

3 tomatoes, peeled and diced

1/2 cup parsley, chopped very fine

salt and pepper

Soak chickpeas overnight, drain, add fresh tap water, and boil until tender. Drain. Prepare cabbage as in 47. Mix all stuffing ingredients with chickpeas and fill cabbage. Arrange stuffed cabbage in cooking pot. Mix lemon juice, mint, and crushed garlic in enough tap water to cover cabbages and cook until tender. Turn over onto serving dish and discard the hard parts that lined the bottom of cooking the pot.

Use same ingredients to make *silq mihshi,* or stuffed chard, substituting brown lentils for chickpeas and omitting the dried mint.

51   Malfuf mihshi — Stuffed cabbage
      Palestine

1 cabbage

30–40 garlic cloves, unpeeled

2–3 tablespoons lemon juice

2 tablespoons cooking fat

meat stock

savory minced meat, 100

Prepare cabbage as in 47. Mix stuffing ingredients with 1 tablespoon cooking fat and fill cabbage leaves. Arrange cabbages in cooking pot, scattering the garlic cloves between the layers of cabbage. Cover with well-seasoned meat stock and remaining cooking oil, weigh down, and allow to simmer over low flame. Turn over onto serving dish, discard the hard parts that lined the bottom of the pot, and sprinkle with lemon juice.

Do not discard garlic. It can be easily pressed out of its outer skin and enjoyed with the cabbage.

Chicken

52   Sharkasiya (Egypt), Cerkez tavuku (Turkey) —
      Chicken cooked Circassian style

2 chickens, about 1 kg each
2 onions, chopped coarsely
a few grains of mastic
a few bay leaves, crushed
10–12 garlic cloves, crushed
1 teaspoon coriander powder
2 loaves of stale bread
1 cup hazelnuts, crushed
2 cups walnuts, crushed
2 tablespoons cooking oil
salt and pepper

This dish is considered the pièce de résistance in any
banquet.

Heat cooking oil, add mastic, stir, cover, and remove
from flame for a few minutes, allowing mastic to melt and
perfume pot. Add chicken, lightly fry, then add onions and
water to cover. Boil until chicken is tender. Remove chicken
from pot, bone, cut into neat pieces, and keep warm.

Sprinkle water on bread to soften, then squeeze to
remove moisture. Crumble.

Mash onions in stock and replace over flame.

Mix garlic, coriander, and seasoning until smooth,
sauté for 3–5 minutes, then toss onto boiling stock together
with nuts and crumbled bread. Adjust seasoning and leave
on slow flame, stirring constantly until sauce becomes like
thin custard. Add chicken pieces, bring to a boil, and serve.

53   Djaj bi-leimoon hamed — Chicken cooked with
        lemon
        Lebanon

    2 chickens, about 1 kg each
    2 onions, sliced thinly
    10–12 garlic cloves, halved diagonally
    1 tablespoon coriander leaves, chopped very fine
    1 tablespoon parsley leaves, chopped very fine
    3 tablespoons lemon juice
    1/2 cup black olives, seeded
    dash of saffron
    cooking oil
    salt and pepper

Cut chicken into neat joints, heat cooking oil, fry lightly, then set aside.

Place onions, garlic, coriander, and parsley in a pot, top with dash of saffron, and leave over very slow flame until they wilt. Add the chicken joints with their cooking oil, seasoning, and 1 cup of hot water. Cover and allow to cook over slow flame, stirring from time to time.

When done, remove chicken joints onto platter, mash vegetables well, add lemon juice and olives, stir, and return to flame to bubble for 2–3 minutes. Pour over chicken joints and serve.

54   Faisinjan — Fried chicken
        Iran

    2 small chickens, about 1 kg each
    1–2 onions, grated
    1 tablespoon walnuts, chopped
    1 cup pomegranate juice
    1 cup chicken broth
    dash of sugar

cooking oil

salt and pepper

Cut chicken into neat joints and fry lightly on all sides, then remove and keep warm.

In the same oil, fry the onions until they wilt, then add walnuts, broth, sugar, pomegranate juice, chicken stock, and seasoning and cook until the sauce thickens. Add chicken pieces and cook over slow flame for another 20–25 minutes.

55   Mussakhan — Chicken roasted with sumac
        Palestine and Jordan

    4 small chickens, about 500–700 g each

    3–4 onions, grated

    2 tablespoons sumac

    3 tablespoons olive oil

    4 loaves of bread

    salt and pepper

Lightly fry onions until they wilt, then mix with sumac, seasoning, and oil. Coat chicken with this mixture and use the rest to stuff the chicken. Roast in the center of a moderate oven, basting occasionally until well browned. When the chicken is nearly ready, place loaves of bread in the same oven to heat. When the chicken is done, open the side of the bread loaf and serve the chicken enfolded in the bread.

56   Djaj mihshi — Stuffed chicken, boiled and fried
        Lebanon

    2 chickens, about 1 kg each

    giblets

    1/2 cup rice

    1 onion, quartered

1 teaspoon cinnamon or nutmeg powder

3–5 grains mastic

cooking oil

salt and pepper

Dice giblets and mix with rice, cinnamon or nutmeg, and other seasonings and stuff into chicken. Sew up openings.

Boil 4 cups of water with onion and seasoning, then lower chicken into pot and cook for 20–30 minutes. Remove and keep warm.

Heat oil and stir in mastic grains for a few seconds before adding chicken. Cover tightly and turn off flame. Allow chicken to absorb fragrance (2–3 minutes) then uncover, turn flame back on, and fry chicken until nicely brown.

Cut up into neat joints, arrange stuffing in middle of serving dish, and surround with chicken joints. The broth may be warmed and used to moisten stuffing.

58 Djaj mihshi — Stuffed chicken, roasted
Lebanon

2 chickens, about 1 kg each

giblets

1/2 cup rice, boiled

1 teaspoon cinnamon or nutmeg powder

1 tablespoon tomato paste

1 tablespoon lemon juice

1 tablespoon olive oil

salt and pepper

Dice giblets and mix with rice, cinnamon or nutmeg, seasoning, and stuff into chicken. Sew up openings.

Dilute tomato paste with lemon juice, add seasoning and oil, and wipe chicken with this mixture inside out. Roast in oven, basting often with the lemon mixture.

Colocasia

59   Colocasia

Colocasia is another name for Jerusalem artichokes or taro.

To prepare colocasia for cooking, peel, cut whatever shape you need and either cook immediately or soak in warm water and vinegar. Rinse in several changes of warm water; this helps colocasia keep its good pink color. Colocasia may also be boiled or roasted in its jacket and peeled afterwards, but the first method is more frequently used.

60   Hrino me colocassi — Colocasia cooked with pork
       Cyprus

1 kg colocasia

1 kg stewing pork

2 onions, chopped

1 cup celery, chopped coarsely

3 tablespoons tomato paste

1 tablespoon lemon juice

corn oil

salt and pepper

Cut colocasia into small cubes and soak in acidulated warm water.

Cut pork into bite-size pieces and lightly fry. Remove pork from pot and fry onions until they wilt, then add celery and tomato paste dissolved in warm water to make 1 1/2 cups. When this boils, add the pork and seasoning and cook for about 10 minutes.

Drain the colocasia, pat dry, and toss into cooking pot with lemon juice. Cover and cook for another 30 minutes.

61 ʻUlʼas matbukh bi-l-khudra — Colocasia stewed with
greens
Egypt

> 1 kg colocasia
> 1/2 kg beef
> 2 onions, quartered
> 1 cup chard leaves, chopped
> 10–12 garlic cloves, crushed
> 1 tablespoon coriander powder
> cooking oil
> salt and pepper

Cut beef into bite-size pieces and parboil with onions.
Add colocasia and seasoning and simmer for 30–40 minutes.

Heat cooking oil, fry crushed garlic—stirring constantly
to prevent it from sticking to the bottom of the pan—add coriander and chard, and cook for 5–7 minutes. Remove from
pan, put in blender with a small amount of meat broth, and
whirl until fully blended. Toss into cooking pot and simmer
for a further 5–7 minutes, adjusting seasoning to taste.

For a richer stew, lightly fry meat, onion, and colocasia
before cooking.

Couscous

62 Couscous bi-l-hut — Couscous with fish
Tunisia

> 1/2 kg couscous (3 cups)
> 1 kg fish fillet
> marinade
>> 2 tablespoons olive oil
>> 1 tablespoon fennel seeds

1 tablespoon caraway seeds

1/2 teaspoon cayenne

1 teaspoon paprika

fish balls

1/4 kg whiting fillets

1 onion, grated

3–5 garlic cloves, crushed

1 egg

1/2 loaf stale bread

1 tablespoon parsley, chopped very fine

dash of harissa, 214

dash of paprika

salt and pepper

mixed vegetables

1 cup chickpeas

2–3 of each of the following: onions (grated); zucchini and carrots (sliced into thin rounds); artichoke hearts (chopped); tomatoes (peeled and
diced)

2 cloves

cinnamon bark

1 teaspoon caraway seeds

cooking oil

salt and pepper

Soak chickpeas overnight, drain, add fresh tap water,
and boil until tender. Drain and reserve liquid.

Mix marinating ingredients and marinate fish for 1–2
hours.

Prepare fish balls: Sprinkle water on bread to soften.
Steam whiting fillets, flake, and mix with a purée of onions,
garlic, paprika, harissa, parsley, beaten egg, bread, and
seasoning. Shape into small balls and fry until brown. Set
aside and keep warm.

Heat oil and brown onions, then stir in zucchini, carrots, and artichokes until well coated with oil. Tie cloves, cinnamon bark, and caraway seeds in a muslin bag and add to onions with boiled chickpeas and enough liquid to completely cover vegetables. Cook on low heat. Sprinkle couscous with cold water, place in perforated steamer over pot, cover, and cook. Uncover once or twice, sprinkle lightly with cold water, and use a fork to separate couscous grains to prevent them from becoming lumpy. Keep over cooking pot until vegetables are tender.

Brush off marinating juice and grill fish on both sides.

Place couscous in serving bowl. Top with grilled fish and fish balls. Serve the cooked vegetables separately.

63   Couscous bi-tamr — Couscous with dates
       Tunisia

> 1/2 kg couscous (3 cups)
> 1/2 kg mutton
> 1/2 kg dates
> 3–4 carrots
> 1–2 turnips
> 5–7 garlic cloves, crushed
> 1 tablespoon harissa, 214
> dash of hot chili
> salt and pepper

Cut meat into bite-size cubes and place in pot. Peel and dice carrots and turnips, add to pot and boil in salted water. When meat is nearly cooked, sprinkle water over couscous and place in steamer over boiling meat for 5–7 minutes. Uncover pot, sprinkle lightly with water, and use a fork to break up lumps of couscous. Remove pits from dates, chop coarsely, add to couscous, and return over boiling meat for further cooking. When both couscous and meat are well cooked, remove from flame and keep separate.

Pour a ladleful of meat broth over garlic, harissa, and chili. Boil over high heat until reduced by half.

Serve couscous, meat, and sauce separately.

64   Couscous bi-lahm — Couscous cooked with meat
Tunisia

1/2 kg couscous (3 cups)
1/2 kg lamb
1/4 kg chickpeas
salt and pepper

Soak chickpeas overnight, drain, add tap water, and boil until tender. Drain and set aside.

Cut lamb into bite-size cubes and boil. When nearly cooked add chickpeas and seasoning. Sprinkle couscous with water and place in a perforated steamer over boiling meat for 5–7 minutes. Remove steamer, break up any lumps with a fork, sprinkle again with cold water, and return over boiling meat for further cooking. When well cooked, sprinkle seasoning over couscous. Serve couscous and meat separately.

65   Maghrabiyeh — Couscous cooked with chicken
Lebanon

1 chicken, about 1 kg
1/2 kg couscous (3 cups)
2 onions, sliced thinly
a few grains of mastic
cooking oil
salt and pepper

Cut chicken into neat joints. Bring onions, mastic, and seasoning to a boil, then add chicken joints and cook. Ten to fifteen minutes before the joints are ready, sprinkle couscous with water and place in a perforated steamer over broth.

Uncover once or twice and break up lumps with fork, sprinkling again with cold water. When couscous is cooked, remove into a deep bowl, keeping warm. Remove chicken joints and fry. Mash onion in broth, thicken, adjust seasoning, and serve separately.

Eggplant

66   Eggplant

There are three types of eggplant. Their usual cooking methods are as follows:

A. Brown and round — roasted, fried, or stewed.

B. Brown, long, and slender — pickled and stuffed.

C. White, long, and slender — stuffed only.

To fry eggplants, slice—peeled or unpeeled—spread on smooth surface, sprinkle with salt, and allow to stand for at least one hour. Squeeze gently to drain moisture, pat dry, deep fry in sizzling oil, then remove onto absorbent paper.

Always roast eggplants in their skins. They can be roasted in a hot oven, but are more commonly roasted on a tin on the stove. When they get tender on one side and juice starts oozing out, turn them over. To prevent their color from changing after roasting, immerse the eggplants immediately in cold water to which lemon juice has been added.

67   Beitinjan mifassakh — Creamy eggplant
Palestine

1 kg brown round eggplant

1/2 cup yoghurt

3–5 garlic cloves, crushed

1 tablespoon parsley, chopped very fine

olive oil

Kibbeh, Syrian style (112)

Opposite: Stuffed vine leaves (194)

Previous page: Kufta flavored with charcoal (107)

Shish kebab, popular throughout the Middle East

Opposite: Grilled lamb (93)

Chopping mulukhiya with a *makhrata*

Opposite: Yoghurt cheese (25) and bread

Following page: Spices and dried hibiscus in a Cairo market

Fry eggplant (see 66). Mash with yoghurt and garlic. Stir in parsley and serve.

68   Hunkar begendi — Creamy eggplant
      Turkey

    1 kg brown round eggplant

    2 tablespoons flour

    2 cups milk, hot

    2 tablespoons cheese, grated

    2 tablespoons parsley, chopped very fine

    2 tablespoons butter

    salt

Roast eggplant (see 66). Drain and mash.

Melt butter and fry flour over very slow flame to a golden color. Remove from flame and stir in hot milk, stirring constantly, then return to flame and allow to bubble. Stir in the eggplant, season, and cook for 10 minutes. Remove from flame, stir in the cheese and chopped parsley, and serve.

69   Imam Biyaldi
      Turkey

The name of this dish in Turkish means literally "the Imam fainted," and is given to several recipes. The original recipe is unknown. Here are three recipes bearing the same name; eggplant is the common ingredient.

    1 kg round brown eggplant

    1/2 kg savory minced beef, 100

    1 cup yoghurt

    3–5 garlic cloves, crushed

    1 tablespoon pine nuts or pecan nuts, chopped

    salt

Fry eggplant (see 66). Place savory minced meat and eggplant in pot over very slow flame and stir frequently until thoroughly blended. Press with wooden spoon on side of pot and drain excess fat. Spread in shallow serving dish to cool.

Add garlic to yoghurt, mix well, and spread over egg-plant mixture, sprinkling with nuts.

70   1 kg brown, slender eggplant

      1 cup olive oil

      1 tablespoon lemon juice

      1 tablespoon tomato paste

      1 teaspoon sugar

      stuffing

          1 cup rice

          2 tomatoes, peeled and diced

          1 onion, grated

          1 cup parsley, chopped very fine

          1/2 teaspoon cinnamon

          salt and pepper

Core eggplants and immerse immediately in salted water. Mix all the stuffing ingredients and fill the eggplants loosely, allowing room for rice to swell. Arrange in pot. Dilute tomato paste and sugar in enough water to cover eggplants, add the oil and lemon juice, and pour over eggplants. Cook over high heat until the liquid boils, then lower heat and simmer until eggplants are well cooked. Serve hot or cold.

71   1 kg brown, slender eggplant

      3 onions, chopped fine

      3 tomatoes, peeled and diced

      1/2 cup parsley, chopped very fine

      1/2 cup olive oil

      1 cup currants

      5 garlic cloves, crushed

      sprig of thyme and bay leaf

      salt and pepper

Soak currants in tepid water. Slice eggplants lengthwise and remove pulp without piercing skin. Dice or mash
pulp and sprinkle with lemon juice. Mix with onions and fry,
then add tomatoes, parsley, spices, and seasoning. Cover
and cook over low heat for about 20 minutes. Remove from
flame and add garlic and drained currants. Mix thoroughly.

Arrange the eggplant skins in a well-greased oven and
fill with the cooked mixture. Sprinkle olive oil over each eggplant half and bake on tray in slow oven.

72   Patlican kizartmasi — Eggplant fritters
      Turkey

    1 kg brown round eggplant
    batter
        1 cup flour
        1/2 cup beer
        salt

Peel eggplants, slice, and sprinkle with salt. Allow to
rest for at least 1 hour. Squeeze and pat dry. Beat batter
ingredients until smooth and dip each eggplant slice in batter. Shallow fry in sizzling oil until tender and golden brown
on both sides.

73   Patlican koftesi — Eggplant/meatballs
      Turkey

    1/2 kg brown round eggplant
    1/2 kg lamb
    1 onion
    2 tablespoons hard cheese, grated
    1 tablespoon flour
    dash of oregano
    dash of sweet basil
    cooking oil
    salt and pepper

Fry eggplants (see 66). Mince twice the meat, onion, spices, and seasoning and lightly fry in the same oil as eggplant. Mash eggplant and add to meat mixture. With wet hands, take a piece of this mixture and roll into a ball the size of a ping-pong ball and set aside on floured surface until you have used all the mixture. Chill balls for 15 minutes before frying in sizzling oil.

74 Sheikh al-mahshi — Eggplant, stuffed
Palestine

> 1 kg brown slender eggplant
> 1/2 savory minced meat, 100
> 2 tablespoons pine nuts
> meat stock or tomato paste
> oil
> salt and pepper

Cut off stem from each eggplant and with sharp knife make a lengthwise slit, leaving 1 cm at both ends. Remove most of the pulp and discard. Place eggplants in salted water until all have been emptied. Drain and pat dry.

Fry eggplants lightly, remove onto absorbent paper, and allow to cool. Add pine nuts to savory minced beef and spoon into fried eggplant shells. Arrange side by side in a baking dish, cover with stock of thinned tomato paste, and bake in preheated moderate oven for 15–20 minutes.

75 Musa''a'a — Stewed eggplant
Egypt, Lebanon, Syria, and Jordan

> 1 kg brown round eggplant
> 1/2 kg savory minced beef, 100 or 101
> 2 cups tomato juice
> cooking oil
> salt and pepper

Fry eggplant (see 66). Line the bottom of a baking dish with half the eggplant slices, spread savory minced beef on top, and cover with the remaining half of the eggplant slices. With the tip of a knife make several deep dents in the eggplants. Season tomato juice and pour over eggplant. Bake in center of moderate oven for about 30 minutes.

In Lebanon and Syria, pine nuts are added to the savory minced beef.

Fish

76 Samak bi-tahina — Fish baked in tahina sauce
Palestine

1–2 kg white fish
2 tablespoons flour
2 onions, sliced very thin
bay leaf and cardamom
1 cup tahina, 156 or 157
2 tablespoons lemon juice
1 tablespoon vinegar
1/2 teaspoon cumin powder
5–7 garlic cloves, crushed
olive oil
salt and pepper

Coat fish in seasoned flour and fry in sizzling oil. Remove onto absorbent paper, cool and flake, and place in baking dish. With the same oil, fry onions until golden, drain, and add to fish.

Boil fish bones and skin with seasoning, cardamom, and bay leaf for 15 minutes. Strain in fine sieve, preferably lined with muslin, and cool.

Blend tahina, lemon juice, vinegar, cumin, garlic, salt
and about 1 to 1 1/2 cups of cooled fish broth until thin and
well blended. Pour over fish and bake in moderate oven for
20–30 minutes.

77   Samak bi-salsat al-tamata wa-l-sabbar — Fish
      baked in tomato sauce and tamarind
      Gulf States

    1 fish, about 1 1/2 kg
    2 onions, sliced very thin
    2 tablespoons tamarind paste (soaked and strained to
        form 1/2 cup of liquid)
    2 tomatoes, peeled and diced
    2 green peppers, sliced very thin
    1/2 cup coriander leaves, chopped
    1 teaspoon coriander powder
    1 teaspoon cumin
    1 teaspoon mixed spices
    3 tablespoons lemon juice
    3 tablespoons tomato paste
    7 garlic cloves, crushed
    dash of ginger powder
    olive oil
    salt

Slit open fish lengthwise from head to tail (as if
opening a book).

Dissolve tomato paste in the tamarind juice and set
aside.

Mix garlic, lemon juice, mixed spices, and half the
fresh coriander and blend well. Set aside half this mixture
and rub the fish with the rest. Allow to rest.

Grease oven tray, place fish (rubbed with mixture
above), and bake until well cooked.

Fry onions and pepper until they wilt, then stir in remaining spice mixture and place over baked fish. Top with fresh coriander and tamarind juice and leave in oven 5–7 minutes until fish absorbs the aroma of the juice and onion mixture.

78   Hut moqli — Fried fish
        Tunisia

        1 kg fish fillets
        2 onions, chopped very fine
        2 zucchinis, sliced into thin rounds
        5 garlic cloves, crushed
        2 tablespoons tomato paste
        1–2 eggs, well beaten
        1 cup bread crumbs, powdered
        2–3 tablespoons lemon juice
        1/2 teaspoon harissa, 214
        olive oil
        salt and pepper

Marinate fish in lemon juice and salt. Fry onions and zucchini lightly, then add garlic, harissa, seasoning, and tomato paste diluted in 1 cup of water and cook for 15 minutes. Mash and boil again to reduce volume and thicken sauce.

Dip fish fillets in beaten eggs, coat with bread crumbs, and deep fry. Place on serving dish and top with tomato sauce.

79   Sharmolit badinjan — Grilled fish with eggplant
        Tunisia

        1 kg fish fillet
        1 kg brown round eggplant, fried (see 66)
        2 onions, chopped very fine

5 garlic cloves, halved diagonally

2 tablespoons tomato paste

1/2 teaspoon harissa, 214

1/2 teaspoon tabil, 213

2 tablespoons cider vinegar

olive oil

salt

Fry eggplant (see 66). Grill fish and set aside, keeping it warm. Brown onion in same oil as eggplant, add garlic, harissa, tabil, and tomato paste diluted in 1 cup of water and cook over medium heat for 15 minutes, stirring often. Mash eggplant with vinegar and seasoning and stir into the tomato sauce. Cook for another 3–5 minutes, then pour over grilled fish and serve.

80 Sayadiyyeh — Stewed fish
Jordan

1–2 kg fish

3–5 onions, chopped coarsely

7–10 garlic cloves, crushed

1 teaspoon cumin powder

1 teaspoon cinnamon powder

3 tablespoons lemon juice

2–3 cups rice

salt and pepper

Marinate fish in lemon juice and salt for 1–2 hours.

Fry onions until thoroughly brown. Stir in garlic and fry, stirring constantly to prevent sticking. Remove from flame and mash well with the backside of a spoon, then add spices, seasoning, and plenty of water. Return to flame, bring to a boil, then add fish and cook until tender. The broth should be very dark. Set aside some of the broth to barely cover fish and use the rest to cook the rice.

Heat oil and fry rice until all grains are well coated with oil. Add broth to form 1 1/2 times volume of rice, adjust seasoning, and cook until tender. Serve rice and fish stew separately.

81   Samaka haara — Fish, stuffed and baked
Iraq

1–2 kgs white fish
2 onions, chopped fine
5 garlic cloves, crushed
2 tablespoons lemon juice
1/2 cup bulgur
1 cup walnuts, crushed
1/2 cup pomegranate seeds
1 tablespoons parsley, chopped very fine
1 tablespoon coriander leaves, chopped very fine
salt

Soak bulgur for 1 hour. Pound or whirl in electric blender the bulgur, garlic, onions, walnuts, parsley, and coriander until well blended. Add pomegranate seeds and stuff fish with this mixture. Place fish and any extra stuffing in a well-oiled oven dish, cover with foil, and bake in a preheated oven for 30 minutes on high heat, then lower heat and allow fish and mixture to cook in moderate heat for another 30 minutes.

82   Tagin samak bi-l-firik — Fish casserole with hulled grain
Egypt

1 kg fish
5–7 garlic cloves
2 cups hulled grain
1/2 teaspoon cumin

1–2 tablespoons flour

oil

salt

Coat fish with flour, fry, then remove onto absorbent paper to cool. Skin, bone, and flake into large chunks. Boil skin, bones, and trimmings of fish with cardamom and seasoning for 15 minutes. Strain in a very thin sieve.

Using the same oil used for frying the fish, lightly fry the hulled grain, then cover with the stock formed above, adding more water if necessary to produce 5 cups, and add cumin and garlic. Cook for 10 minutes. Remove from flame and place in casserole dish, burying fish flakes in the grain. Bake in preheated oven for 30 minutes.

Liver

83   Kibda meqliyeh — Fried liver
Lebanon

1 kg liver

2 onions, chopped very fine

5–7 garlic cloves, crushed

1/2 teaspoon mint powder

1 tablespoon vinegar

2 tablespoons flour

dash of mixed spices

2 cups hot water

cooking oil

salt and pepper

Slice liver and coat with seasoned flour. Heat oil and fry onions until they wilt, then add garlic and fry, stirring constantly to prevent sticking. Add hot water, vinegar, mint, mixed spices, and other seasonings and boil over high heat, then lower heat to cook further.

In another pan, fry liver slices on both sides, then toss into the broth produced above and cook for another 5 minutes.

84   Ciger tavasi — Fried liver
      Turkey

1 kg liver
2 spring onions, chopped very fine
2 tablespoons parsley, chopped very fine
2–3 tablespoons plain flour
cooking oil
salt and pepper

Soak liver in salted water for 30 minutes. Drain, pat dry, and cut into 3-cm cubes. Coat with seasoned flour and fry until nicely brown. Be careful not to overcook. Sprinkle with seasoning and top with spring onions and parsley. Toss to mix.

85   Kibda mishwiyeh bi-toom — Grilled liver with garlic
      Lebanon, Syria, and Jordan

1 kg lamb liver
7–10 garlic cloves, crushed
1 teaspoon dried mint powder
1/2 cup olive oil
lemon juice
salt and pepper

Soak liver in salted water for 30 minutes. Drain, pat dry, and cut into 3-cm cubes. Mix garlic with mint and coat liver with the resulting paste, then brush with oil and allow to rest for 1 hour in a cool place.

Skewer liver and grill over glowing charcoal for 2–3 minutes on each side, being careful not to overcook. Baste with the marinating juice.

To serve, sprinkle with lemon juice and seasoning.

86   Kirsheh — Liver and kidney stew
Yemen

1/2 kg liver
1/2 kg kidney
2 onions, sliced very fine
10 garlic cloves, crushed
6 tomatoes, peeled and diced
1 teaspoon turmeric
1 teaspoon coriander powder
1 teaspoon cumin powder
3 cardamom seeds, smashed open
dash of ginger powder
cooking oil
salt and pepper

Wash kidney, remove skin, chop coarsely, and soak in several changes of water. Drain and pat dry. Cut liver into small cubes. Mix garlic with turmeric, cumin, coriander, and cardamom until a thick paste is formed.

Heat oil and fry kidney, stirring constantly, and leave on flame until juice is reabsorbed. Remove from flame and fry onions in the same oil until they wilt, then lower heat to the minimum, add ginger and garlic mixture, and cook for 3 minutes further, stirring constantly. Return kidney to flame, raise heat, add liver, and cook for 7–10 minutes, while still stirring. When the liver looks brownish, add tomatoes and seasoning and cook for about 5 minutes, or until tomatoes are cooked.

Meat Dishes

87 Kinds of meat

Though most of these recipes call for lamb, with the exception of a very few, mutton, beef, or veal work equally well. Obviously, your choice of meat will depend on availability and individual taste.

88 Magbus al-lahm — Mutton and rice
Gulf States

1 kg mutton
3 cups rice
1/2 cup chickpeas
2 cinnamon stalks
2–3 black pepper corns
2–3 cloves
dash of turmeric
2–3 garlic cloves, sliced very thin
2–3 whole garlic cloves
2 tablespoons lemon juice
1 onion, grated
1 teaspoon mixed spices
2–3 grains cardamom, smashed open
1/2 cup rose water
ghee
1–2 tablespoons almond slivers
salt and pepper

Soak cinnamon stalks in rose water.

Soak chickpeas in water for 2–3 hours, drain, add tap water, and boil until tender.

Cut mutton into bite-size cubes and boil with enough water to barely cover, skimming when necessary. When all the scum has been removed from the surface of the liquid, add the cinnamon stalks (previously soaked, and saving their liquid), cloves, turmeric, garlic slices, seasoning, and half the grated onion. Cover with plenty of water, so that when the meat is tender there will be about 5 cups of stock. Remove mutton from stock.

While mutton is cooking, place the rest of the grated onion with salt in a pot over slow flame, stirring to prevent it from sticking to bottom of pot. When the onion browns, add ghee, mixed spices, garlic, almonds, cardamom, and drained rose water and leave on slow flame for about 10 minutes.

Add lemon juice to crushed garlic and coat mutton pieces with this mixture. Heat ghee and fry mutton lightly. Add to onion mixture.

Heat more ghee and fry rice until all the grains are well coated with ghee. Add the 5 cups of meat stock and cook uncovered on high heat until the stock is evaporated. Make a well in the middle, add the mutton mixture, cover, and allow to cook over very slow flame for 20–30 minutes, or until the rice is tender.

To serve, fold rice into mutton mixture and mix well.

89   Fatta al-ra'ba — Fatta with neck of lamb
Egypt

"Fatta" literally means tossing pieces of bread into a liquid. The most popular fatta is prepared with neck of lamb, but rabbit, poultry, or other cuts of meat work just as well.

2 kg neck of lamb

2 onions, quartered

5–6 cardamom seeds, bashed open

5–6 grains mastic

2 cups cooked rice

15–20 garlic cloves, crushed

2 tablespoons vinegar

4 loaves crisp local bread

butter

salt and pepper

Ask the butcher to cut the neck at each vertebrae; this way you will get neat, uniform pieces.

Boil water with onion, cardamom, mastic, and seasoning, then add neck and cook until tender. Remove neck and keep warm. Discard cardamom and mash onion until completely disintegrated. Return to flame to boil.

Fry garlic in butter until golden, stirring constantly to keep it from sticking to the bottom of the pan. Add vinegar and boil for 3 minutes, then pour over boiling broth and simmer for 3 minutes.

Cut up bread into bite-size morsels and place in serving bowl. Ladle in some boiling broth to moisten bread thoroughly, then cover with a thick layer of rice. Wet the rice with remaining broth and arrange lamb pieces on top.

90   Fattit firakh — Chicken fatta
      Egypt

Same ingredients and preparation as 89 above, but substitute chicken for neck of lamb and include heavily garlic-flavored yoghurt as a side-dish.

91   Mansaf — Lamb cooked in yoghurt
      Lebanon, Jordan, and Syria

2 kgs lamb neck

3 onions, chopped very fine

2 tablespoons pine nuts

1 tablespoon turmeric

1/2 teaspoon cinnamon

1/2 teaspoon mixed spices

3 cups yoghurt

2 egg whites

2 loaves crisp bread

2 cups cooked rice

ghee

salt and pepper

Ask your butcher to cut the neck at each vertebrae so that you get neat, uniform pieces. Boil lamb in cold salted water, skimming whenever necessary, until tender.

Fry pine nuts until golden, remove, and set aside. Fry onion in the same oil until golden, then toss the fried onions with turmeric, mixed spices, and cinnamon into the pot with the boiling lamb and allow to simmer for 5 minutes.

Beat egg whites until frothy, add to yoghurt, and beat again. Pass yoghurt through sieve into cooking pot, adjust seasoning, and boil uncovered for another 5 minutes.

Break bread into bite-size pieces and place in bottom of serving bowl. Wet with some broth, cover with rice, top with remaining yoghurt, and arrange lamb all around. Sprinkle with pine nuts.

92   Seleq — Boiled leg of lamb
Gulf States

leg of lamb

2 onions, chopped very fine

2 cups of hot milk

2 cups rice

1 cup ghee, melted

salt and pepper

Place leg of lamb in a pot with onions and seasoning and boil until tender. Remove lamb and keep warm. Mash onions in broth, add milk and rice, and boil until rice is well cooked and mushy. Place in serving dish, sprinkle with the melted ghee, and cover with warm leg of lamb.

93   Shawerma (Lebanon), Gass (Iraq), and Doner ke-
      bap (Turkey) — Grilled lamb

Although there are different names for this dish, the
recipe is exactly the same way in all these countries.

even-sized rounds of boneless lamb

Marinate lamb in olive oil, vinegar, grated onion,
thyme, oregano, and seasoning for 4–6 hours.

Load a long, heavy spit with the meat, interspersing
layers of meat with slices of fat from the tail of the lamb. Fit
the bottom of the spit with a disc to keep the meat in place
and place it in front of a vertical fire with an electrically
driven motor. The spit revolves and the outer layer of the
shawerma gets grilled evenly. Use a very sharp knife to slice
off the outer layers of the grilled meat. Serve hot in local
bread.

94   Oozi — Roast lamb
      Gulf States

To serve this dish to an honored guest is considered
the epitome of Arab hospitality.

1 small lamb, headless

1 tablespoon turmeric

1 tablespoon mixed spices

1 tablespoon cumin powder

1 tablespoon coriander powder

1 teaspoon ginger powder

2 tablespoons lemon juice

10 garlic cloves, crushed

1 cup rose water

1 teaspoon saffron

2 *loomi*,* crushed

mixture of 1/2 cup each of tamarind juice, rose water,
     and water, plus 2 tablespoons mixed spices

stuffing

> 5–6 cups rice (depending on size of lamb)
> 1 cup chickpeas
> 10–12 hard-boiled eggs (depending on number of
>   guests)
> 2 cups of a mixture of almonds, pistachios, and
>   pine nuts
> 2 cups grated onion
> 10 garlic cloves
> 1 tablespoon turmeric
> 5 cinnamon stalks
> 10 cardamom, smashed open
> 2 tablespoons coriander leaves, chopped very fine
> ghee, or any animal fat, for basting
> salt and pepper

Wash lamb inside and out and dry well. Mix all ingredients (except stuffing) and coat lamb with this mixture inside and out, cover, and allow to absorb aroma.

Soak chickpeas overnight.

To prepare the stuffing, first parboil rice and chickpeas in water with cinnamon, cardamom, and salt. Drain and discard cinnamon and cardamom, but retain boiled liquid.

Place onions in a pot over flame and stir constantly, sprinkling with water to prevent sticking. When the onions brown, add 3 tablespoons ghee, rice, chickpeas, some of the above liquid, mixed spices, lemon juice, nuts, and rose water, cover, and allow to simmer for 10 minutes over medium flame. Remove from flame and stir in coriander leaves. Shell hard-boiled eggs, keeping them whole, and add to the mixture above. Now stuff lamb with this mixture, sew up all openings, and roast either over an open charcoal fire or in an oven for 4–6 hours, according to weight of lamb, basting often with the marinating juice to keep meat moist.

To serve, remove thread and empty stuffing. Never slice oozi—cut it up or tear it into chunks and serve with stuffing separately.

* Loomi are limes dried out in the sun and used to flavor food or boiled as medicine.

95   Tajeen ma'doones — Lamb stewed with parsley
        Tunisia

    1/2 kg lamb
    2 onions, grated
    1/2 cup dried white beans
    2 tablespoons tomato paste
    1 tablespoon bread crumbs
    1 cup parsley leaves, finely chopped
    3 tablespoons hard cheese, grated
    4 eggs
    1/2 teaspoon tabil, 213
    1/2 teaspoon cayenne
    olive oil
    salt and pepper

Soak beans overnight, drain, add fresh water, and boil for 20–30 minutes. Drain and reserve liquid.

Cut lamb into bite-size cubes and roll in seasoning. Fry onions until they wilt, add lamb, and fry until juices are reabsorbed. Add cayenne, beans, seasoning, and tomato paste dissolved in enough of the beans' boiling liquid to just cover lamb, and cook until lamb and beans are tender. Remove from flame.

Beat eggs and mix with parsley, bread crumbs, cheese, and seasoning and add to lamb mixture, stirring to blend thoroughly. Pour this mixture into a well-greased casserole dish and bake in moderate oven for 15–20 minutes.

96   Tajeen na'na' — Lamb stewed with mint
        Tunisia

        1/2 kg lamb
        2 onions, grated
        1/2 kg tomatoes, peeled and diced
        1 teaspoon tabil, 213
        6 eggs
        1/2 cup bread crumbs
        1 tablespoon mint powder
        3 tablespoons grated cheese
        ghee
        salt and pepper

Cut lamb into bite-size pieces and roll in seasoning.

Heat ghee and fry onions until golden, then add lamb and brown until juices are reabsorbed. Stir in tomatoes, seasoning, and spices and cook over slow flame for 30 minutes, adding hot water if the liquid does not cover the meat. Strain the meat and set aside the broth. Place meat in greased casserole.

Beat eggs and mix with cheese, mint, bread crumbs, and seasoning. Add the meat and 1 cup of the above broth and place in a well-greased casserole dish and bake in moderate oven for 20 minutes.

97   Tava* — Lamb stew
        Cyprus

        1 kg lamb
        3 onions, chopped coarsely
        5–7 tomatoes, peeled and diced
        1 tablespoon tomato paste
        1 teaspoon cumin powder
        salt and pepper

Cut lamb into bite-size cubes. Dilute tomato paste in 1/2 cup of warm water and place in casserole with all the ingredients. Close with tight-fitting lid and bake in moderate oven for 2–3 hours, or until lamb is tender and sauce thickens.

* A *tava* is an unglazed terracotta casserole dish with tight-fitting lid. This dish is only prepared in the *tava* and thus bears its name.

98   Kebab halla — Stewed meat
Egypt

1 kg beef
2 onions, chopped finely
1 teaspoon cinnamon
2 tablespoons flour
5–7 garlic cloves, crushed
cooking oil
salt and pepper

Cut beef into bite-size cubes. Mix flour, cinnamon, and seasoning and roll meat in this mixture. Cook meat, onion, and pinch of salt over very slow flame. When the juice is re-absorbed, add garlic and cooking oil and fry lightly. Add water to barely cover and cook over low heat for 1 hour, adding more hot water, along the side of the pot, whenever the level of the juice is too low. Serve with the juice, which should be fairly concentrated.

99   Ground meat dishes

Cuts of meat marbled with fat are best for minced beef to use for kufta or for stuffing vegetables. If these are not available, add fat to the meat while mincing. The fat prevents the kufta from becoming dry and imparts a better flavor to the stuffed vegetables.

100 Lahma mu'assaga — Savory minced meat (1)
Egypt

1 kg beef
2 onions, chopped very fine
cooking oil
salt and pepper

Mince the beef coarsely. Fry the onions until pale gold, then add beef and seasoning and cook until the juice is reabsorbed.

101 Lahma mu'assaga — Savory minced meat (2)
Egypt

1 kg beef
1 onion, chopped very fine
1/2 cup tomato juice
1/2 teaspoon mixed spices
cooking oil
salt and pepper

Mince the beef coarsely. Place meat, onion, mixed spices, and seasoning over low flame, stirring often. When the juice has been reabsorbed, add tomato juice and cook until the juices are substantially reduced. Add cooking oil and cook for 5 minutes.

102 Kabaar — Meatballs, fried
Tunisia

1/2 kg lean lamb
2 onions
5–7 garlic cloves
2 potatoes
1/2 teaspoon cinnamon powder
2 tablespoons parsley leaves

2 tablespoons coriander leaves

2–3 tablespoons bread crumbs

2–3 eggs

cooking oil

salt and pepper

Boil potatoes until very tender, peel, and mash. Mince twice lamb, onions, garlic, parsley, coriander, and seasoning and mix with mashed potatoes, bread crumbs, cinnamon, and well–beaten eggs. Shape into small meatballs and chill for 30 minutes before frying in sizzling oil.

103   Kafta — Meat patties, fried
Palestine

1 kg lamb

1 cup parsley leaves

2 onions

2 eggs

1 small tomato, peeled (optional)

cooking oil

salt and pepper

Mince twice meat, parsley, onions, and tomato (if used) with seasoning. Beat eggs, add to meat, and knead well until very thoroughly mixed. Shape into patties about 5–7 cms in diameter and 2 cms thick and fry in sizzling oil.

104   Kafta mabrumeh (Syria), Kafta mkabtaleh
       (Lebanon) — Meatballs, baked

Only the name differs; the ingredients and methods of cooking for these dishes are the same.

1 kg lamb

2 onions

5–7 garlic cloves

2 eggs

3–4 tablespoons pine nuts

cooking fat

salt and pepper

Mince twice meat, onions, garlic, and seasoning. Beat eggs, add to meat, and knead well. On a flat, lightly greased surface, roll out meat to a thickness of about 1 cm. Cut into rounds and place some pine nuts in the middle of each round, then roll. Place in well-greased oven tray, brush each roll with cooking fat, and bake in middle of moderate oven for 30 minutes. Then place under grill to brown, shaking pan to grill the rolls evenly.

105 Fatteet kafta madqooqeh — Meat patties, fried
Lebanon

1 kg lamb

1 tablespoon mint leaves

2 loaves dry bread

10 garlic cloves, crushed

2–3 cups rich yoghurt

1/2 teaspoon dried mint powder

cooking oil

salt and pepper

Mince twice lamb, mint, and seasoning. Shape into patties and fry until nicely brown.

Break bread into bite-size morsels and place in a deep serving bowl.

Mix yoghurt, garlic, and mint powder. Stir the cooking oil left over from the fried patties into the yoghurt and pour over bread. Top with kafta.

106   Kafta sajieh — Meat patties, fried
       Jordan

    1 kg lamb
    1 tablespoon mint
    10 garlic cloves, crushed
    1 cup milk
    2 loaves unleavened bread
    1 cup yoghurt
    1/2 teaspoon mint powder
    cooking oil
    salt and pepper

Prepare as in 105, but soak bread morsels in hot milk before adding yoghurt mixture and kafta.

107   Kufta bi-l-fahma — Meat fingers flavored with char-
       coal
       Egypt

    1 kg beef
    3 onions
    1 tablespoon lemon juice
    2 tablespoons parsley
    cooking fat
    salt and pepper
    1 piece charcoal

Mince twice beef, onions, and 1 tablespoon parsley, then add lemon juice, and seasoning and knead well. Shape into fingers about 5–7 cms long and 2 cms thick. Grease cooking pot and arrange kufta neatly side by side. Brush kufta fingers very lightly with cooking oil and repeat with other layers of kufta, brushing with fat until all the kufta is used. Cook over very slow flame until the meat loses all its juice, then increase heat to maximum to reduce juice. Shake the pot gently several times to check that the meat fingers are all well fried and do not stick to bottom of pot. Have ready a piece of burning-red charcoal. Make a well in the middle of pot, toss in the charcoal, cover, and allow to simmer for 3–5 minutes longer. Remove charcoal and serve on a bed of parsley.

108　Kufta bi-l-kurrat — Meatballs with leeks
Egypt

> 1 kg beef
> 2 small leeks
> 2 eggs
> 1 tablespoon bread crumbs
> 2 tablespoons lemon juice
> cooking oil
> salt and pepper

Boil leeks in salted water until tender, then drain and squeeze gently to extract all moisture. Mince beef and leeks twice, add beaten eggs, bread crumbs, and seasoning and knead. Shape into small balls and fry, shaking pan often to brown meatballs evenly. Remove onto absorbent paper.

Strain the remaining cooking oil into a pot, add two cups of water and the lemon juice, and bring to a boil. Gently drop in the meatballs and simmer for 30 minutes, shaking pot to prevent meatballs from sticking to the bottom.

109　Izmir koftesi — Meatballs cooked in tomato sauce
Turkey

> 1 kg beef
> 3 onions
> 2 thick slices stale bread
> 1 egg
> 2 tablespoons parsley
> 5–7 garlic cloves

1 teaspoon cumin powder

1 tablespoon flour

cooking oil

salt and pepper

sauce

    2 cups tomato juice

    dash of sugar

    1 sweet green pepper, diced very fine

    salt and pepper

Sprinkle bread with cold water, then squeeze to extract excess moisture. Add all ingredients to bread—except eggs, flour, and cooking oil—and mince twice. Break eggs and knead into mixture. With wet hands, shape into round or oval balls and roll in seasoned flour to coat very thinly.

Heat cooking oil and lightly fry meatballs, then remove onto absorbent paper. In the same oil fry the green pepper until it wilts, then add tomato juice, sugar, and seasoning and cook for 10–12 minutes. Return meatballs to pot and simmer in tomato sauce for 30 minutes, allowing sauce to thicken.

110   Kuftat ras al-'asfur — Meatballs with ground rice
       Egypt

1 kg beef

2 onions

1/2 cup ground rice

2 cups tomato juice

1 teaspoon vinegar

1 teaspoon sugar

cooking oil

salt and pepper

Mince beef and one onion twice. Add ground rice and seasoning and knead thoroughly. With wet hands, shape into small round balls (ras al-'asfur means literally "head of sparrow," denoting the size of the meatballs), heat oil and fry. Remove onto absorbent paper

Chop the remaining onion and fry in the same oil as the meatballs. Dissolve sugar in tomato juice, add vinegar, pour over fried onions, and cook for 15 minutes. Return meatballs to the cooking pot and simmer over low heat for 20 minutes longer, shaking pot gently to prevent the meatballs from sticking to the bottom.

111　Kibbeh — Meat ground with bulgur
　　　Syria, Lebanon, and Jordan

> 1 kg lamb, free of all fat
> 3 onions, quartered
> 2 cups bulgur, fine
> salt and pepper

Soak bulgur for 1 hour in warm water.

Mince meat with onions three times, adding small cubes of ice every now and then to give the meat more texture. Drain bulgur and mince another three times with meat and seasoning. Kibbeh must have the consistency of soft dough.

This is the basic recipe of kibbeh, the most popular dish in the countries mentioned above.

112　Kibbeh shamiyeh — Kibbeh, Syrian style
　　　Syria, Lebanon, and Jordan

> kibbeh, 111
> savory minced beef, 100
> pine nuts
> ghee

Mix savory minced beef with pine nuts.

With wet hands, take a small piece of kibbeh, place in the moist palm of your hand, and with the index finger of the other hand make a hole in the kibbeh and rotate it, half closing your palm until the kibbeh becomes very thin. Half fill the hole with well-spiced savory minced beef and a small dot of fat. Moisten your hand again and close the kibbeh to form a round or oval ball.

Heat ghee and fry kibbeh, shaking pan often to brown kibbeh all over. You can also place the kibbeh in a greased oven dish, dot each ball with some ghee, and bake them, shaking the dish every now and then until the kibbeh browns evenly.

113   Kibbeh labaniyeh — Kibbeh cooked with yoghurt
Lebanon, Syria, and Jordan

kibbeh shamiyeh, 112

1/2 cup chickpeas

2–3 cups yoghurt

1 egg white

1 teaspoon mint powder

Soak chickpeas overnight, drain, add fresh water, and parboil for 5–7 minutes. Drain.

Prepare kibbeh shamiyeh but do not fry. Place in cooking pot with chickpeas. Beat egg white until frothy, stir into yoghurt to stabilize it, then pass through sieve onto kibbeh and cook uncovered for 1 hour. Sprinkle with mint and serve hot or cold.

114   Kibbeh bi-l-suniyeh — Kibbeh, baked
Lebanon, Syria, and Jordan

kibbeh, 111

savory minced beef, 100

pine nuts

cooking fat

With wet hands, flatten out some of the kibbeh 2 cms thick to line the bottom of a well-greased oven dish. Spread savory minced meat mixed with pine nuts over kibbeh. Again with wet hands, flatten out more kibbeh, thinner than before, i.e., approximately 1 cm thick, to cover minced beef completely. Wet the tip of a knife, release kibbeh all around, then cut up kibbeh into 6–8 sections. Wetting the tip of the knife again, make rectangular or oblong incisions in upper layer only. Dot each section with a knob of cooking fat and bake in preheated moderate oven until top browns, about 30–45 minutes.

Okra

115 Okra

To prepare, wash and dry okra well. Peel ridges very thinly, then peel the cap by turning okra around a knife, removing the hard edges. The top of the okra should then look conical.

116 Bamya murag — Okra stew
Iraq

1 kg okra

1/2 kg mutton

4 garlic cloves, sliced thinly

3 tablespoons tomato paste

1 tablespoon tamarind (soaked and drained to make
1/2 cup)

1 tablespoon lemon juice

dash each of cumin, coriander, cinnamon, cloves, and
peppercorns

ghee

salt and pepper

Prepare okra as in 115.

Cut mutton into bite-size cubes and boil with spices until tender. Remove from pot, saving broth.

Heat ghee and fry mutton, then add okra and garlic and stir until it is all well fried. Dissolve tomato paste in tamarind and add with broth to cooking pot and simmer for 30 minutes. Remove from flame and stir in lemon juice.

117   Bamya weeka — Mashed okra
       Egypt

       1 kg okra
       1/2 kg ground beef
       2 onions, sliced very fine
       2 cups tomato juice
       1 tablespoon ta'liya, 152
       cooking oil
       salt and pepper

Prepare okra as in 115. Fry onions until golden, add ground meat, and fry until juices are reabsorbed. Season tomato juice and pour over the frying meat. Cook for 10 minutes, then lower heat, add okra, and simmer, stirring constantly until all the ingredients are completely blended. Add ta'liya and simmer for 5 minutes longer.

118   Bamya weeka sa'idi — Mashed okra, Upper Egyptian style
       Egypt

       1 kg okra
       1/2 kg beef
       2 cups meat stock
       2 hot peppers, finely chopped
       1 tablespoon ta'liya, 152
       cooking oil
       salt and pepper

Prepare okra as in 112.

Cut meat into bite-size cubes and boil in stock for 20–30 minutes, or until tender. Remove meat from stock, add okra and peppers, and cook for 10 minutes, then mash with a fork. Return meat to mashed okra in cooking pot with ta'liya and simmer for 5 minutes longer..

Pastries

119   Ajeen — Pastry, basic recipe
Palestine

1 kg best-quality flour
1 teaspoon sugar
1 tablespoon active dry yeast
1/2 cup ghee or melted butter
1/2 cup oil
salt

Cream yeast with sugar in warm water and leave to bubble in warm place. Sift flour with salt and add yeast and enough water to form a soft dough. Knead thoroughly, beating to allow plenty of air to penetrate the dough.

Cut up the dough into balls the size of small marbles. Combine ghee or melted butter with oil. Take one ball at a time, dip fingertips in oil mixture, and spread dough thinly by hand on smooth, greased surface. Reroll and spread again 2–3 times, moistening fingers in oil each time. Flatten out into squares on greased tin and allow to rise for about 1 hour before using.

Sfeeha — Pastry with meat filling (1)
Palestine

pastry, 119

120   Filling A

    1 cup savory minced beef, 100
    2 tablespoons pine nuts
    1 1/2 cups yoghurt

121   Filling B

    1 cup savory minced beef, 100
    2 tablespoons raisins
    1 cup thin tahina sauce, 156

Lightly fry pine nuts until golden or lightly fry raisins until they puff. Mix the ingredients of the desired filling.

With fingertips, press down pastry in 2 or 3 places and spread around the filling, allowing 1 cm of dough all around to keep the filling from spreading beyond the pastry. Bake in preheated hot oven until the pastry becomes crisp and crusty.

122   Tagin lisan 'asfur — Pastry casserole
    Egypt

    1/2 kg lisan 'asfur*
    1/2 kg beef
    2 onions, sliced very thinly
    2 sweet green peppers
    1 teaspoon cinnamon
    1–2 cups meat stock
    1 tablespoon butter
    1 tablespoon oil
    salt and pepper

Cut meat into bite-size cubes. Remove stems and seeds from peppers and slice thinly. Sauté onion and peppers in a mixture of butter and oil, then add meat and fry until the juice is reabsorbed/evaporated. Add stock to cover, toss in peppers, cinnamon, and seasoning and cook for 15 minutes. With a perforated skimmer, remove all these ingredients and place in an earthenware casserole dish. Reboil stock and add lisan 'asfur and parboil for 5–7 minutes, then pour over meat mixture. If the stock does not completely cover, add more hot water. Bake in preheated moderate oven for 30 minutes.

* Dry, small, oval-shaped pastry. Lisan 'asfur literally means "swallow's tongue," thus eloquently describing its shape and size.

123   Sabanikhiyat — Spinach turnovers
Egypt

pastry, 119
filling
    1 kg spinach
    2 onions, chopped very fine
    2 tablespoons lemon juice
    2 1/2 cups oil
    salt

Rinse spinach leaves, sprinkle with salt, and rub to extract juice. Rinse again, shake off moisture, then chop very finely. Add chopped onions, lemon juice, and 2 cups of oil. Mix thoroughly.

On a floured surface, roll out dough thinly and cut into rounds about 10 cms in diameter. Place a spoonful of spinach in the center of each round, wet the edges with water, and lift the pastry on three sides and press together to form a pyramid. Lightly brush with oil, place on greased oven tray, and bake in preheated moderate oven until the dough is crisp and golden.

124   Fatayer bi-l-sabanekh — Spinach turnovers
Syria

pastry

    3 cups best-quality flour

    1 teaspoon active dry yeast

    1 teaspoon baking soda

    1/2 teaspoon sugar

    1/2 teaspoon salt

    1/2 cup yoghurt

    2 tablespoons olive oil

filling

    1/2 kg spinach

    2 tablespoons parsley

    3 onions, grated

    1 tablespoon sumac

    3 tablespoons lemon juice

    2 tablespoons walnuts, chopped

    salt and pepper

Cream yeast and sugar in 1/2 cup warm water. Sieve flour, salt, and baking soda, add yeast, and stand for 15–20 minutes. Knead, adding oil and yoghurt alternately until the dough is smooth and leaves the sides of the pot clean. Cover and keep in a warm place for at least 1 hour.

Rinse spinach leaves, sprinkle with salt, and rub to extract juice. Rinse, shake off moisture, then chop very fine. Add parsley, onion, sumac, lemon juice, olive oil, nuts, and seasoning and mix thoroughly.

On a floured surface, roll out the dough thinly, and cut into rounds about 10 cms in diameter. Place a spoonful of spinach in the center of each round, wet the edges with water, and lift the pastry on three sides and press together to form a pyramid. Lightly brush with oil, place in a greased oven tray, and bake in preheated moderate oven until dough is crisp and golden.

125   Sambusek bi-l-jibneh — Turnovers with cheese filling
Lebanon

pastry, 119
filling

   1 cup grated white cheese
   2 tablespoons parsley, chopped very fine
   2 hard-boiled eggs
   cooking oil

Mash eggs and mix with cheese, parsley, and seasoning.

On a floured surface, roll out the dough thinly and cut into rounds about 10 cms in diameter. Place a spoonful of the cheese mixture in the center of each round, wet the edges with water, and lift the pastry on three sides and press together to form a pyramid. Lightly brush with oil, place in a greased oven tray, and bake in preheated moderate oven until dough is crisp and golden.

126   Sambusek bi-l-lahmeh — Turnovers with meat filling
Lebanon

pastry, 119
filling

   1/2 kg lamb
   2 onions
   2 tablespoons pine nuts
   salt and pepper
   cooking fat

Mince meat and onions and fry until the juices are reabsorbed/evaporated. Season and add pine nuts. Allow to cool.

On a floured surface, roll out the dough thinly and cut into rounds about 10 cms in diameter. Place a spoonful of meat filling in the center of each round, wet the edges with

water, and lift the pastry on three sides and press together
to form a pyramid. Lightly brush with oil, place in a greased
oven tray, and bake in preheated moderate oven until dough
is crisp and golden.

127   Shushbarak — Pastry filled with meat and cooked in
      yoghurt
      Palestine

> 2 cups flour
> 1/2 kg lean beef, minced
> 1 onion, chopped very fine
> 2 tablespoons pine nuts
> 1/2 teaspoon mixed spices
> 1/2 teaspoon cinnamon powder
> 4-5 cups yoghurt
> 2 egg whites
> 7–10 garlic cloves, crushed
> ghee, salt and pepper

Sift flour and salt into mixing bowl and add enough
water to knead it into a smooth dough that leaves the sides
of the bowl clean. Allow to rest for 1 hour.

Fry pine nuts until golden, remove, and set aside. Fry
onions in the same oil until they wilt, then add meat and fry
until the juices are reabsorbed. Stir in pine nuts, seasoning,
and spices and mix thoroughly.

Roll out pastry on lightly floured surface and cut into
rounds. Place 1/2 teaspoon of the meat mixture on pastry
and with wet fingers close dough crescent-shaped, then wrap
crescent around one finger and press the edges into a hat-
shape. Place on a well-greased oven tray and lightly brush
each shushbarak with ghee. Bake in moderate oven until
crisp and golden.

Fry garlic in a small amount of ghee until golden, stirring constantly to keep it from sticking to the bottom of the

pot, then add mint and mix. Beat eggs until frothy, add to yoghurt, and blend well. Place yoghurt in uncovered pot over low flame, add garlic mixture, stir well, and, when bubbling, add shushbarak and cook for another 7–10 minutes.

128   Asabi' gullash bi-l-lahma — Dry pastry fingers with meat filling
Egypt

gullash*
savory minced beef, 100 or 101
butter

Cut gullash sheets into 10-cm squares and keep covered with moist cloth. Taking one square at a time and covering the rest immediately, place on a smooth surface and arrange minced meat in a narrow strip at the center of the square 1 cm from both ends. Fold ends over the meat mixture and roll tightly so that it resembles a cigarette. Arrange tidily in a greased baking tray, brush top with melted butter, and bake in preheated moderate oven until golden.

    * Paper-thin dough sold in bakeries. Gullash dries out quickly and should be kept covered.

129   Ru'a' bi-l-gibna — Crisp pastry with cheese filling
Egypt

ru'a'*
chicken broth
butter
filling
    equal amounts of
    a) salted hard cheese (e.g., Balkan), grated
    b) skimmed cheese
    hard-boiled eggs
    1 fresh egg, beaten
    pepper

Mash skimmed cheese and hard-boiled eggs and mix with beaten egg, grated cheese, and pepper.

Grease baking tray and boil stock. Take one layer of ru'a' at a time, dip in boiling broth, and line bottom of tray. Sprinkle with butter and repeat to cover bottom with 3–4 layers. Spread cheese mixture evenly and repeat, dipping ru'a' in broth and sprinkling with butter for another 3–4 layers. Sprinkle top with remaining melted butter and bake in preheated moderate oven. When the top browns, turn over to allow the bottom to brown too. Cut into sections while still hot.

* Very thin cracker-type bread.

130   Ru'a' bil-l-lahma — Crisp pastry with meat filling
Egypt

ru'a'
savory minced beef, 100 or 101
meat broth
butter

Proceed as in 129, substituting meat filling for cheese.

131   Sha'riya — Vermicelli
Egypt

1/2 kg vermicelli
2 tablespoons butter
1 teaspoon oil
chicken broth

Heat cooking pot well before adding butter and oil. When melted and bubbling, add vermicelli and fry until deep gold, stirring constantly. Heat well-seasoned chicken broth and cover vermicelli. Lower heat and allow vermicelli to get tender, about 5–7 minutes.

Rice

132   Rice

Rice is always measured by volume, not by weight. The amount of water or stock used varies with the type of rice, but unless indicated on the package a rough ratio of 1 cup rice to 1 1/2 cups water is a good rule. If the rice needs to be rinsed, cook it immediately afterward as the rice spoils if washed and left to dry.

133   Ruzz mifalfil — Rice, fried
Egypt

> 2 cups rice
> 3 cups water
> cooking oil
> salt

Heat oil and fry rice, stirring to coat all grains with the oil. Add water and salt, stir, and leave uncovered until water is absorbed/evaporated. Cover, lower heat to the minimum, and allow slow cooking.

134   Ruz bi-djaj — Rice and chicken pilaf
Lebanon

> 2 chickens, about 1 kg each
> 2 cups rice
> 1 onion, quartered
> 1 tablespoon pine nuts
> 1 tablespoon almonds
> 1/2 teaspoon nutmeg
> ghee
> salt and pepper

Bring water, nutmeg, onion, and seasoning to a boil, then add chicken and cook until the chicken is tender. Re-

Stuffed zucchini cooked in yoghurt (205)

Opposite: Zucchini grilled (202)

Previous page: Vegetables on display in a Cairo market

White bean stew (46)

Opposite: Fattush (146)

Stuffed artichoke (42)

Opposite: Eggplant fritters (72) and Imam Biyaldi (69)

Meatballs cooked in tomato sauce (109)

move from broth and mash onion. Skin and bone chicken, setting aside the large pieces, and return the small pieces to the broth.

Lightly fry pine nuts and almonds until golden and set aside. In the same oil fry the large chicken pieces until golden, then remove and set aside. Fry the rice in the same oil, stirring constantly until all grains are well coated with oil, then add the stock (which should be about 5 cups) with the small chicken pieces, and cook until the rice is tender.

To serve, heap rice in the serving dish, decorate with golden nuts, and surround with chicken pieces.

135   Patlicanli pilav — Eggplant pilaf
       Turkey

  2 cups rice
  1 kg brown eggplant, round or slender
  2 medium onions, sliced very thin
  4 tomatoes, peeled and diced
  1/2 cup parsley, chopped very fine
  1/2 cup mint leaves, chopped very fine
  oil, salt and pepper

Dice eggplant without peeling, sprinkle with salt, and allow to rest for one hour. Squeeze out moisture, pat dry, and fry until lightly brown. Remove from flame onto absorbent paper and fry onions in the same oil until they wilt. Stir in tomatoes, seasoning, parsley, mint, and eggplant and bring to a boil. When boiling, add rice and enough water to cover. Boil over quick flame, then reduce heat and simmer gently for 30 minutes.

136   Mu'addas — Rice with lentils
       Gulf States

  2 cups rice
  1/2 cup split or brown lentils

1 onion, chopped very fine

ghee

salt

Heat ghee and fry onions until they wilt. Add rice and lentils and stir well until all the grains are well coated with oil. Add about 4 cups of water with seasoning and boil uncovered over high heat until the water is absorbed/evaporated. Cover and allow very slow cooking.

137   Ic pilav — Rice pilaf with nuts
       Turkey

2 cups long-grain rice

1/2 kg chicken livers

3 cups chicken stock

2 tablespoons pine nuts

3 spring onions, chopped

2 tablespoons currants

2 tablespoons dill, chopped very fine

dash of allspice

butter

salt and pepper

Chop livers and soak in salted water for 1 hour. Drain. Fry pine seeds until golden, remove, and set aside. With the same oil fry the onions until they wilt, then add liver and fry for 5–7 minutes. Remove from heat and add allspice.

Fry rice stirring until all grains are coated with butter, add chicken stock, currants, dill and seasoning. Stir, cover, and cook for 20 minutes. Remove cover, stir in liver and pine nuts, cover again and cook for 30 minutes or until rice is tender.

138   Ruzz bi-l-mukassarat — Rice, fried with nuts
      Egypt

2 cups rice
2 onions, chopped very fine
3 cups broth
1/2 cup boiled gizzards
1/2 cup livers
1 tablespoon almond slivers
1 tablespoon raisins
1 tablespoon pine nuts
1 tablespoon sugar
1 teaspoon nutmeg
1 teaspoon cinnamon
cooking oil
salt and pepper

Fry onions until rich brown. Drain, mash with the back of a spoon until completely disintegrated, then add to broth with one teaspoon of cinnamon and seasoning.

Fry the rice in the same oil as the onions, stirring constantly until all grains are well coated with oil, then add broth and cook until tender.

Soak liver in salted water for 1 hour, drain, pat dry, and fry for 5–7 minutes. Lightly fry the pine nuts and almond slivers, then remove and set aside. Fry the raisins until they puff and add them to the pine nuts, nutmeg, sugar, remaining cinnamon, liver, and gizzards. Toss well to mix.

Place nut mixture in a cake mold, cover with the cooked rice, then turn over onto serving dish.

139   Mashkul — Rice with onions
      Gulf States

2 cups rice
2 onions, chopped very fine

ghee

salt

Bring 4 cups of water to a boil, add rice and salt, and allow to cook for 10 minutes, breaking up with a fork once or twice to keep the rice from getting lumpy. Remove from flame, drain, and spread to separate.

Heat ghee and fry onions until golden. Remove from flame, set aside half the onions and ghee, and return the rest to the flame to fry until rich brown. Add the boiled rice and stir the onion into the rice, cover with 2 cups of hot water, and allow to cook uncovered. When the liquid is reabsorbed, place the golden onions on top, sprinkle with the set-aside ghee, cover, and allow slow cooking.

140   Ruz ahmar — Rice with onions
        Egypt

2 cups rice

2 onions, chopped very fine

1/2 teaspoon cumin

2-3 garlic cloves, crushed

oil

salt

Fry onions until they wilt, then add garlic and cumin and fry, stirring constantly until rich brown. Remove from flame and with the back of a spoon mash until completely disintegrated. Add rice and fry until all grains are well coated with oil, then add 3 cups of hot salted water, cover, and allow to cook over moderate flame until tender.

This dish is usually served with fish.

141   Ruz bi-sabanekh — Rice cooked with spinach
        Palestine

2 cups rice

1 kg spinach

1/2 cup chickpeas

2 onions, chopped very fine

olive oil

salt and pepper

Soak chickpeas overnight, drain, add fresh water, and boil until tender. Drain.

Prepare spinach as in 177.

Fry onions until golden, then add rice and seasoning and fry, stirring constantly until each grain is coated with oil. Stir in spinach and chickpeas and add 3 cups of hot water, cover, and cook over moderate heat for 30–40 minutes or until rice is tender.

142 Ruz bi-l-sha'riya — Rice, fried with vermicelli
Egypt, Lebanon, Syria, and Jordan

2 cups rice

1/2 cup vermicelli

cooking oil

salt

Heat oil and fry vermicelli until rich gold, then add rice and stir constantly to coat all grains with oil. Add 3 cups of water plus salt and leave uncovered until water is absorbed/evaporated. Cover, lower heat to the minimum and allow slow cooking.

143 Kibbet halab — Rice balls, fried
Iraq

2 cups rice

1 teaspoon saffron

1/2 kg ground beef

1/2 cup slivered almonds

1/2 cup celery, chopped very fine, or parsley

1/2 teaspoon mixed spices

dash of tumeric soaked in 1 tablespoon of rose water

1 egg

2 tablespoons raisins

1–2 tablespoons flour

ghee

salt and pepper

Boil rice in 4 cups of water with saffron and salt until tender, breaking up any lumps with a fork. If the water is not completely absorbed, strain, then add lightly beaten egg and, with fingers dipped in rose water, knead to form soft, shapeable dough.

Fry beef, then add celery or parsley, almonds, mixed spices, and seasoning and cook together over slow flame for 10 minutes.

Take a small amount of the rice dough in the palm of your hand, moistening it with rose water, and with the other finger make a hole and rotate, half-closing palm. Fill with ground beef mixture and, again with moistened palm with rose water, close rounds to form oval balls. Place on floured surface until all the dough has been used. Deep fry.

144   Cheloo Dig — Steamed crusty rice
Iran

2 cups long-grain rice

1 cup yoghurt

2 tablespoons ghee

salt

Wash the rice in boiling water and drain. Bring 8 cups of heavily salted water to a boil, add washed rice, and cook for 5 minutes. Drain and rinse in hot water.

To one cup of half-cooked rice, add the yoghurt and stir well. In a heavy-based pan, swirl a tablespoon of melted butter to coat the base and sides. Add the rice/yoghurt mixture. Place on flame with the remaining rice to steam on top.

Sprinkle the remaining ghee over the steaming rice and cook over moderate flame, breaking up any clusters that form.

To serve, place steamed rice in the center of the serving dish and break up the crusty rice that was cooked in the base of the pan and arrange it all around.

Salads

145 Salatit shamandur — Beetroot salad
Lebanon

> 1 kg beetroot
> 1 tablespoon vinegar
> 5–7 garlic cloves, crushed
> 1/2 teaspoon sugar
> salt

Wash and brush beets to remove any grit and boil until tender. Remove from pot, setting aside about 2 tablespoons of boiled water and discarding the rest.

Slice or chop beets and place in serving bowl. Dilute sugar and salt in the water set aside above, add vinegar and garlic, mix, and pour over beets.

146 Fattush — Bread salad
Palestine and Jordan

> 3 loaves bread, stale and dry
> 2–3 cucumbers, diced
> 2–3 tomatoes, diced
> spring onions
> 1 sweet green pepper, chopped fine
> 1/2 cup parsley leaves, chopped
> 1/2 cup coriander leaves, chopped
> 5–7 garlic cloves, crushed

2–3 tablespoons lemon juice

1 teaspoon sumac

2–3 tablespoons olive oil

salt

Break bread into bite-size morsels, sprinkle with water to soften, and place in deep serving bowl. Add all the vegetables. Mix lemon juice, olive oil, sumac, garlic, and salt and pour over vegetables. Toss to mix together.

Other fresh vegetables (i.e., lettuce or radishes) can be added to this salad, but its most important feature is the lemony taste produced by the sumac and lemon juice.

147   Tabuleh (Lebanon), Kisir (Turkey) — Bulgur salad

1/2 kg bulgur

5–6 spring onions, chopped very fine

1 cup parsley leaves, chopped

1/2 cup mint leaves, chopped

4 tomatoes, peeled and diced

4 cucumbers, peeled and diced

3 tablespoons lemon juice

3 tablespoons olive oil

baby raw vine leaves or lettuce leaves

salt

Soak bulgur for 1 hour. Drain and place in a deep serving bowl with onions, parsley, mint, tomatoes and cucumber. Mix lemon juice with olive oil and salt and pour over salad. Toss to mix.

The traditional way to eat tabuleh is to hold a raw vine or lettuce leaf with thumb, index, and middle fingers and scoop some tabuleh into the leaf—never using cutlery.

148   Cacik (Turkey), Salatit zabadi (all Arab countries) — Cucumber salad

1/2 kg cucumbers
1–2 cups yoghurt
7–10 garlic cloves, crushed
1 teaspoon powdered mint
salt

Peel cucumbers, cut into rounds, place in strainer, sprinkle lightly with salt, and let them sit a while to lose their excess moisture. Pat dry and place in serving bowl. Stir the garlic into the yoghurt and pour over cucumbers. Stir gently, then sprinkle with mint powder.

149   Salatit al-fuleyfileh mishwiyeh — Grilled green pepper salad
Tunisia

5–6 green peppers
5 garlic cloves, crushed
1/2 teaspoon cumin
2 tablespoons lemon juice
salt

Chill the sweet peppers, remove skins, stems, and seeds, and chop coarsely. Mix garlic, cumin, lemon juice, and salt and pour over peppers.

150   Ispinak — Spinach salad
Turkey

1 kg fresh spinach
2 onions, chopped very fine
2 tablespoons olive oil
1/2 cup parsley, chopped very fine
2 tablespoons *beyaz peynir* (feta cheese)
salt and pepper

Rinse spinach, chop coarsely, and heat in a pot to wilt. Drain in colander, pressing down with a spoon to remove moisture. Place in bowl.

Fry onion until golden and combine with other ingredients, tossing to mix thoroughly.

Sauces

151 Skorthalia — Garlic sauce

Cyprus

10 garlic cloves, crushed

2 tablespoons white vinegar

1 tablespoon lemon juice

2 tablespoons olive oil

2 tablespoons almonds, crushed

chunk of stale bread

salt and pepper

Sprinkle water on bread to soften, then squeeze out excess moisture. Crumble in serving bowl.

Soak garlic in vinegar for 10 minutes before adding to bread with almonds and seasoning. Beat in the lemon juice and oil alternately in thin streams until the sauce becomes thick and custard-like.

152 Ta'liya — Fried garlic

Egypt

20 garlic cloves, crushed

1 tablespoon ground coriander

cooking oil

Mix garlic, coriander, and seasoning until smooth, then sauté for 3–5 minutes. Toss into pot of boiling stew; a spoonful of the cooking broth back into the frying pan, stir and toss again into your cooking pot, thus ensuring that all the ta'liya is used.

153   Tarator — Hazelnut sauce
       Turkey

       1 cup hazelnuts, ground
       1 chunk stale bread
       3–5 garlic cloves, crushed
       1 cup olive oil
       2 tablespoons white vinegar
       salt

Sprinkle bread with water to soften, then squeeze out excess moisture. Crumble in bowl and add almonds and garlic. Beat in lemon juice and oil alternately in thin streams to reach the consistency of thin custard. Chill before using.

Though this is the original tarator, a combination of ground nuts, pine nuts, almonds, and/or walnuts can be substituted for the hazelnuts, in which case lemon juice is used instead of vinegar.

154   Sharmula — Sauce for grilled meat
       Gulf States

       2 onions, slice very thin
       5–7 garlic cloves, crushed
       1 tablespoon parsley, chopped
       1 tablespoon coriander, chopped
       dash of ginger powder
       dash of saffron powder
       dash of cumin
       dash of hot pepper
       cooking oil
       salt

Heat cooking oil and add ginger, saffron, cumin, and hot pepper and cook for 1–2 minutes. Lower heat and add onions, garlic, parsley, and coriander and cook—stirring constantly—until the sauce is well blended.

This sauce goes especially well with game and camel.

155　Kishk — Milky cold sauce
Egypt

> 2 cups chicken broth
> 1/2 cup flour
> 1 cup milk
> 1 onion, sliced very thin
> 1 tablespoon butter
> salt and pepper

Mix flour and seasoning. Mix chicken broth with milk and pour over flour mixture, stirring to blend. Place over low flame and cook, stirring constantly, until it reaches the consistency of thin custard. Cool in a shallow serving dish.

Fry onion until nicely brown. Drain on absorbent paper to cool and use to decorate the sauce.

156　Tahina (all Arab countries), Tahinosalata (Cyprus) — Tahina sauce*

> 1/2 cup tahina
> 2 tablespoons lemon juice
> 1 tablespoon vinegar
> 3–5 garlic cloves, crushed
> salt

Place tahina in mixing bowl, add 2 tablespoons of tap water with all other ingredients, and beat well until smooth.

* Tahina is a paste made from sesame seeds.

157   Tahina — Tahina sauce
        Egypt

   1/2 cup tahina
   2 tablespoons lemon juice
   1 tablespoon vinegar
   3–5 garlic cloves, crushed
   1 small onion, grated
   1 tablespoon parsley, chopped very fine
   1/2 teaspoon cumin powder
   salt

Dissolve salt in 2 tablespoons of water, add cumin, lemon juice, and vinegar, and gradually add tahina—stirring constantly into a paste until smooth.

158   Dim'a misabbika — Cooked tomato sauce
        Egypt

   2 cups tomato juice
   2 onions, chopped very fine
   5–7 garlic cloves, crushed
   1 teaspoon vinegar
   cooking oil
   salt and pepper

Sauté onions until soft, then add garlic and fry until brown, stirring constantly to keep from sticking to the bottom of the pot. Add tomato juice and simmer for 15–20 minutes until the sauce is cooked and its color becomes dark. Add vinegar and seasoning and cook for 2–3 minutes longer.

   Almost all recipes for stewed vegetables call for this sauce, whether cooked with meat or not.

159   Saltsa tomata — Tomato sauce
       Cyprus

    3 tomatoes, peeled and diced
    2 tablespoons tomato paste
    1 onion, chopped very fine
    1 teaspoon sugar
    bay leaf and cinnamon bark
    cooking fat
    salt and pepper

Heat oil, fry onion until golden, then add diced tomatoes and cook for 3–5 minutes. Dilute tomato paste with an equal amount of water, add to cooking pot with the rest of the ingredients, and cook uncovered for 20 minutes, allowing sauce to thicken. Discard bay leaf and cinnamon bark.

160   Bazha — Walnut sauce
       Turkey

    1 cup walnuts, crushed
    5–7 garlic cloves, crushed
    2 tablespoons white vinegar
    2 spring onions, chopped very fine
    1 tablespoon mint powder
    1 tablespoon parsley, chopped very fine
    salt and pepper

Mix all the ingredients, together with an additional 2 tablespoons of water, until smooth.

This sauce usually accompanies fried meatballs.

Soups

161 Tbikha — Barley soup
     Tunisia

     1/2 cup pearl barley
     1/2 kg lamb
     3 onions, grated
     5–7 garlic cloves, crushed
     2 tablespoons tomato paste
     1/2 teaspoon fennel seeds
     1 teaspoon mixed spices
     1 tablespoon *hrous,* 209
     cooking oil
     salt and pepper

Boil pearl barley until tender in three times their measure in water. Remove from flame and set aside.

Fry onions until they wilt, add tomato paste, fennel seeds, garlic, mixed spices, and hrous and stir over flame for 3–5 minutes.

Cut lamb into bite-size cubes and add to cooking pot with just enough water to cover. Allow to cook over slow flame until lamb is very tender and most of its juice is gone. Add the barley (with its liquid), adjust seasoning, and serve.

162 Shurba bi-l-tarbiya — Chicken soup with eggs and
     lemon (1)
     Egypt

     6–8 cups chicken soup
     2 egg yolks
     2 tablespoons lemon juice

Set aside a ladleful of cold soup and boil the rest. Put egg yolks in tureen and stir in the cold soup, blending thoroughly. Immediately before serving, add one ladleful of boiling soup at a time to the egg mixture, stirring thoroughly until all the soup has been used. Stir in the lemon juice and serve.

Work quickly—this soup cannot be reheated.

163   Shurba bi-l-tarbiya — Chicken soup with eggs and lemon (2)
Egypt

6–8 cups chicken soup

2 egg whites

2 tablespoons lemon juice

Set aside a ladleful of cold soup and boil the rest.

Beat eggs until frothy, then add lemon juice and cold soup. Stir until well blended.

When soup is nearly boiling, add the egg mixture and cook on low flame, stirring to thicken, but do not allow soup to boil.

164   Leblebi — Chickpea soup
Tunisia

2 cups chickpeas

1 onions, chopped

1 bone marrow

5–7 garlic cloves, crushed

1 teaspoon cumin

3 tablespoons lemon juice

2 loaves stale bread

dash of harissa, 214

olive oil

salt and pepper

Soak chickpeas overnight, drain, add fresh water, onion, and bone marrow and boil until chickpeas are tender. Shake marrow into soup and mash with onion. Season.

Heat oil and fry garlic and harissa, stirring constantly to prevent them from sticking to the bottom of the pot. Add chickpeas and broth and cook for 5 minutes. Remove from flame and stir in the lemon juice and cumin.

Cut bread into bite-size morsels, place in serving bowl, and top with the chickpea soup. Serve immediately.

165   Dugun corbasi — Festive soup
       Turkey

> 1/2 kg lamb
> 1 onion, grated
> 1 carrot, diced very finely
> 2–3 cups rich meat broth
> 2 egg yolks
> 1–2 tablespoons lemon juice
> 1 tablespoon flour
> cooking oil
> salt and pepper

Cut lamb into bite-size cubes, roll in seasoned flour, and fry. Add to broth, bring to a boil, and toss in carrot, onion, and seasoning and simmer for about 1 hour. Remove the meat, set aside one ladleful of soup, and mash the vegetables into the soup. Return meat to soup and keep over very low flame.

Beat eggs and stir in lemon juice. Add the cooled ladleful of soup to eggs, then beat very well. Pour egg mixture into remaining soup for 2–3 minutes. Do not allow the soup to boil or the eggs will curdle.

166   Shurba bi-l-hut — Fish soup
       Tunisia

> 1 kg white fish, filleted
> head, backbone, tail and trimmings of fish
> 1 cup pearl barley

1–2 onions, chopped coarsely

5–7 garlic cloves, halved diagonally

1 teaspoon cumin powder

1 teaspoon coriander powder

1/2 cup celery, leaves and stalk chopped coarsely

1 tablespoon parsley, chopped

2 tablespoons tomato paste

2 tablespoons lemon juice

2 tablespoons olive oil

dash of paprika

salt and pepper

Place head, backbone, tail, and trimmings in a pot with enough water to cover. Boil, skimming whenever necessary.

Lightly fry the fish fillets. Remove and set aside. Using the same oil, sauté the onions until they wilt, then add tomato paste and stir for 2–3 minutes. Add to the pot of boiling fish parts, together with garlic, cumin, coriander, parsley, celery, and seasoning. Boil for 20 minutes. Cool, remove fish parts, whirl the liquid in a blender, and strain in a very thin sieve (preferably lined with muslin). Return to pot, add fish fillets, adjust seasoning, and boil for 7–10 minutes or until the fish is cooked. Add lemon juice and serve.

167   Psarosoupa avgolemono — Fish soup with eggs and lemon
Cyprus

1–2 kgs fish heads, backbones, and trimmings

2 onions, chopped coarsely

3 carrots, sliced into rounds

1/2 cup celery, stalks and leaves chopped

1/2 cup parsley, chopped

1/2 cup rice

2 eggs

2 tablespoons lemon juice

salt

Place fish heads, backbones, and trimmings in a pot with plenty of water and boil, skimming whenever necessary. Add all vegetables and seasonings and simmer for 30 minutes, or until the vegetables are very tender. Remove fish parts, strain in very thin sieve (preferably lined with muslin), adjust seasoning, and return to flame. Add rice and cook until rice is tender. Keep soup boiling over a low flame.

In a serving tureen, beat the eggs until frothy, then add lemon juice—stirring constantly in one direction. When well mixed, ladle boiling soup into bowl in small amounts, continuing to stir in the same direction. Serve immediately.

168   Shurbet al-ras — Sheep's head soup
Palestine

1 sheep head

1 onion, chopped coarsely

1 carrot, sliced into rounds

3–4 celery stalks, chopped coarsely

10 garlic cloves, crushed

bay leaf

4–5 cardamom seeds, smashed open

2 tablespoons parsley, finely chopped

yoghurt

croutons, salt, and pepper

Break the skull lengthwise and soak in several changes of salted water. Singe off hairs and scrape with a blunt knife. Wash under running water and remove brain. Cover with water and boil, then discard boiled water. Add fresh water to cover, along with onion, carrot, celery, bay leaf, cardamom, garlic, and seasoning and bring to a boil. Simmer for 60–90 minutes. Remove from flame, bone, and cut meat and tongue into small neat pieces. Mash vegetables well into soup and return to flame, adding the meat and adjusting seasoning. Boil for 3–5 minutes longer, adding more hot water if necessary. Remove from flame and stir in the parsley.

To serve, place a few croutons in the bottom of individual serving plates, add 1–2 tablespoons of yoghurt, and top with very hot soup.

169   Tshurba — Hearty soup
Gulf States

> 1 kg mutton cutlets
> 2–3 cubes of mutton tail
> 1–2 onions, chopped coarsely
> 1–2 tomatoes, peeled and diced
> 2–3 zucchini, chopped coarsely
> 5–7 garlic cloves, crushed
> 1 cup chickpeas
> 1/2 cup vermicelli
> ghee
> dash of saffron
> salt and pepper

Soak chickpeas in water overnight. Fry cutlets, then add all ingredients except vermicelli, cover with twice their measure in water, and cook until tender. Remove cutlets, mash vegetables, and return cutlets to pot over flame. When the soup boils, adjust seasoning, add vermicelli, and cook for 10 minutes longer, until vermicelli is tender and absorbs the flavor of the soup.

170   Hlalem bi-l-lahm — Hearty noodle soup
Tunisia

> 1 cup hlalem*
> 1/2 kg lamb

1/2 cup chickpeas

1/2 cup fava beans

5–7 garlic cloves, crushed

1 onion, chopped coarsely

1/2 cup celery stalks and leaves, chopped

1/2 cup parsley leaves, chopped

1/2 cup coriander leaves, chopped

2 artichoke hearts, quartered

2 tablespoons tomato paste

2 carrots, peeled and diced

1 cup boiled peas

2 sweet peppers, seeded and chopped

1/2 cup scallions, minced

1 cup spinach leaves (juice squeezed out)

2 tablespoons olive oil

dash of paprika

salt and pepper

Soak chickpeas and fava beans for a few hours. Drain, place in a pot with onions and twice their measure in water, and boil for 15 minutes. Drain and set aside

Cut the meat into bite-size cubes and fry in olive oil, then add scallions and garlic and cook for 5 minutes, stirring constantly. Stir in the tomato paste and cook for 5 minutes longer, then add spinach, celery, parsley, artichoke, carrots, and seasoning and cook, stirring until all the vegetables are well coated with the oil and tomato paste. Add the chickpeas and fava beans with their liquid and simmer for about 30–45 minutes. Allow to cool and skim off any excess fat.

About an hour before serving, return pot to flame, add more salted water if necessary, bring to a boil, add the hlalem and sweet peppers, cover, and simmer until hlalem are plump and soft. Add the boiled peas, adjust seasoning, and sprinkle with fresh coriander.

* Hlalem are home-made noodles.

171   Shurbit 'ads — Lentil soup
       Egypt

   1/2 kg split lentils
   2 onions
   1 tomato
   1 carrot
   1 zucchini
   1–2 tablespoons oil
   1 teaspoon cumin powder
   2 tablespoons lemon juice
   salt

Place lentils, one onion, tomato, zucchini, and carrot in pot and cover with twice their measure in water. Boil over high heat, then lower flame to keep the lentil froth from overflowing. Cook for 20–30 minutes. Remove from flame, cool, and whirl in blender. Strain, then add salt and cumin.

Chop the remaining onion very fine and fry until light brown, then—with its cooking oil—toss into soup and cook for 5 minutes longer. Stir in the lemon juice and serve.

172   Fakes xithati — Lentil soup
       Cyprus

   2 cups brown lentils
   1 cup spring onions, chopped fine
   3–5 garlic cloves, crushed
   2 tablespoons parsley leaves, chopped very fine
   1 tablespoon corn flour
   2 tablespoons vinegar
   2 tablespoons olive oil
   salt and pepper

Place lentils, onions, garlic, oil, and parsley in a large pot with twice their measure in water and boil until tender, then add seasoning. Simmer over low flame. Dilute corn flour in one tablespoon of cold water and pour over boiling lentils to thicken soup. Immediately before serving, adjust seasoning and stir in the vinegar.

173   Tshurbat 'adas — Lentil soup
       Gulf States

    2 cups brown lentils
    1 onion, chopped
    5–7 garlic cloves, crushed
    3 tomatoes, peeled and diced
    2 loomi*
    2 tablespoons vermicelli
    1 teaspoon mixed spices
    2 tablespoons ghee
    salt

Fry the onion until it wilts, then add tomatoes, spices, and garlic and cook for 5 minutes. Place lentils in a pot, add onion mixture, loomi (pierced several times to bring out their flavor), twice their measure in water, and boil until lentils are tender. Remove loomi, add seasoning, vermicelli, and more hot water if needed and cook over low flame, stirring occasionally. Consistency should be that of thick custard.

    * Loomi are limes dried in the sun (pierced several time to release flavor) and used to flavor stews and soups or boiled as medicine.

174   Tshurba bilsen — Lentil soup
       Yemen

    2 cups brown lentils
    1/2 kg bone marrow
    1 onion, chopped

5–7 garlic cloves, crushed

2 tomatoes, peeled and diced

2 tablespoons coriander leaves

2 tablespoons oil

salt and pepper

Boil bones, skimming when necessary. Add lentils and simmer until tender.

Fry onions until they wilt, then add garlic, tomatoes, coriander, and seasoning and cook for 2–3 minutes.

Remove bones from lentils and shake marrow into pot. Add onion mixture and simmer for 20 minutes, stirring occasionally.

175   Yogurt corbasi — Hot yoghurt soup
Turkey

2 cups rich yoghurt

2 onions, chopped finely

2–3 cups chicken broth

1 tablespoon coriander leaves, chopped very fine

cooking oil

salt

Sauté onions until they wilt.

Bring chicken broth to a boil, add onions, and simmer for about 10 minutes. Remove from flame and gradually pour yoghurt into broth, stirring constantly. Return to flame and heat until just at the boiling point. Remove from flame, add salt, and sprinkle with coriander.

176   Eshkene shirazi — Yoghurt soup
Iran

2–3 cups yoghurt

2 onions, chopped very fine

2 tablespoons flour

1 tablespoon fenugreek

2 tablespoons chopped walnuts

cooking oil

salt and pepper

Grind fenugreek into powder. Fry onions until golden, then add flour and cook over very low flame until well blended. Add walnuts and fenugreek, with 1/2 cup of hot water, and stir until smooth. When well blended, add 2 cups of hot water and seasoning and simmer for 30 minutes.

Stir one ladleful of hot soup into yoghurt, beat well, then toss this mixture into hot soup over flame; remove immediately before boiling.

Spinach

177   Spinach

Spinach has a very strong taste and puts some people's teeth on edge. An easy way to modify the taste is to chop the spinach coarsely, sprinkle lavishly with cooking salt, and rub. The spinach will thus lose some of its juice and become more palatable. Rinse again.

178   Di''iyit sabanikh — Baked spinach
Egypt

1 1/2 kg spinach

1/2 kg beef, minced

2 onions, chopped very fine

7–10 garlic cloves, halved diagonally

2–3 cups tomato juice

1/2 cup chickpeas

cooking oil

salt and pepper

Soak chickpeas overnight, drain, add fresh water and boil until tender. Drain.

Fry onions until well browned, add meat and fry until the juice is completely reabsorbed/evaporated. Add one cup of tomato juice, cook for 10 minutes, and place in bottom of cake mold.

Prepare spinach as in 177. Sauté spinach in small amount of oil until it wilts and discard any excess liquid. Mix with boiled chickpeas, garlic, and seasoning and place on top of meat. Top with remaining tomato juice and bake in preheated moderate oven for 30 minutes. Turn over onto platter before serving.

179   Ispanak kavurmasi — Spinach with yoghurt sauce
       Turkey

       1 kg spinach

       2 onions, chopped very fine

       5–7 garlic cloves, crushed

       2 tablespoons olive oil

       1/2 cup yoghurt

       salt and pepper

Prepare spinach as in 177. Place in pot over low flame and allow to wilt. Drain in colander. Press to extract all moisture.

Heat olive oil and fry onions until pale brown. Add spinach and seasoning and cook for 10 minutes. Remove onto serving bowl.

Mix yoghurt with garlic and stir into spinach. Serve cold.

180   Shula kalalambar — Spinach cooked with lentils
       Iran

       1 kg spinach

       1 cup brown lentils

3–4 garlic cloves, crushed

1/2 teaspoon cumin powder

1/2 teaspoon coriander powder

butter

salt and pepper

Prepare spinach as in 177. Place in pot over low flame and allow to wilt. Drain in colander, pressing down to extract all moisture.

Boil lentils until tender, drain, and add to spinach. Mix well.

Melt butter, add vegetables, spices, and seasoning and cook for 5–7 minutes longer.

181   Sabanikh matbukha — Stewed spinach
Egypt

1 1/2 kg spinach

1/2 kg beef

2 onions, chopped

1/2 cup hulled grain or split chickpeas

1–2 tablespoons lemon juice

salt and pepper

Prepare spinach as in 177. Place in pot over low flame and allow to wilt. Drain. Press to extract all moisture.

Soak hulled grain or split chickpeas in warm water for 15 minutes, drain, add fresh water, and boil for 10 minutes. Drain and set aside.

Cut beef into bite-size cubes. Fry onions until they wilt, then add beef and fry until the juice is reabsorbed/evaporated. Add hulled grain or split chickpeas, water to cover, and cook for 15 minutes. Add spinach, adjust seasoning, and cook for another 20 minutes. Turn off flame and stir in the lemon juice.

For variety, substitute tomato juice for water and omit lemon juice.

182   Nokhod — Stewed spinach with chickpeas
Iraq

1 kg spinach
1 cup chickpeas
1/2 cup lentils
1 onion, chopped very fine
5 tomatoes, peeled and diced
1 tablespoon lemon juice
1 tablespoon dill, chopped very fine
cooking oil
salt and pepper

Soak chickpeas overnight, drain, add fresh water, and boil until tender. Drain and set aside.

Prepare spinach as in 177. Place over low flame and allow to wilt. Drain. Press to extract all moisture.

Fry onions until they wilt, then add lentils, spinach, and tomatoes and cook over very low flame until lentils are very tender (add hot water whenever necessary). Add boiled chickpeas, seasoning, dill, and lemon and cook for another 5 minutes.

Tomatoes

183   Yesil dolmates bastisi — Green tomatoes gratin
Turkey

1 kg green tomatoes
2 onions, sliced
2–3 tablespoons hard cheese, grated
1/2 cup stock
olive oil
salt and pepper

Fry the onions until they wilt, then spread to line the bottom of an oven-proof dish. Slice the tomatoes thickly and place over onions. Mix the stock with the remaining oil and seasoning and pour over vegetables. Cover dish with foil and bake in low heat in the oven until tomatoes are tender. Mash the vegetables, adjust seasoning, and stir in the grated cheese, Place under grill to brown top.

184   Yakhnet bandura — Stewed tomatoes
       Palestine

    1 to 1 1/2 kg ripe tomatoes, peeled and diced
    1/2 kg beef
    3 onions, sliced
    3–4 cardamom seeds, smashed open
    bay leaf
    cooking oil
    salt and pepper

Cut beef into bite-size cubes. Heat cooking oil and fry onions lightly, then add spices tied in muslin bag. Add meat cubes and fry until juices are evaporated. Add hot water to cover and cook until meat is tender. Discard bag, mash onions, add diced tomatoes, and simmer for 15–30 minutes.

185   Tamatim mahshiya — Stuffed tomatoes
       Egypt

    12–15 firm round tomatoes
    2 tablespoons tomato paste
    salt and pepper
    stuffing
        1/2 cup rice
        2 tablespoons dill, chopped very fine
        2 onions, chopped very fine
        salt and pepper

Slice tops off tomatoes and scoop out pulp, saving the tops for later use. Mash pulp and mix with the rest of the stuffing ingredients and fill tomatoes, allowing room for rice to swell. Replace tops and arrange tidily upright in greased oven dishes. Dilute tomato paste and sugar in 1–2 cups water, add vinegar and seasoning, and pour over stuffed tomatoes. Cook in moderate oven for 30 minutes.

186   Tomates yemistes — Stuffed tomatoes
       Cyprus

> 12–15 firm round tomatoes
> 1 onion, grated
> 1 cup rice
> 1 tablespoon pine nuts
> 2 tablespoons raisins
> 2 tablespoons parsley, chopped very fine
> 2 tablespoons mint, chopped very fine
> dry white wine
> 1/2 teaspoon sugar
> olive oil
> salt and pepper

Slice tops off tomatoes and scoop out pulp, saving the tops for later use. Place pulp in saucepan with seasoning and a dash of sugar and simmer until soft. Mash or press through sieve.

Gently fry onion until golden, then add pine nuts and cook for 2 minutes. Sir in rice, raisins, parsley, mint, and hot water to cover and cook for 5 minutes, until liquid is absorbed.

Fill tomatoes with this mixture, allowing room for rice to swell. Replace tops and stand in oven dish. Mix the puréed tomato pulp with an equal amount of wine. Pour over tomatoes and cook in moderate oven for 30 minutes.

Mixed Vegetables

187   Mixed vegetables

Stuffed mixed vegetables are very popular all over the Middle East. The Turkish name *dolmeh* is also used in many Arab countries. Dolmeh, or dulma, refers to stuffing with meat, whereas *yalandji* refers to meatless stuffing. Here are three recipes for the stuffings used for mixed vegetables.

A. Minced beef and rice (equal quantities of both), salt, and pepper.

B. Minced beef and rice (equal quantities of both) with grated onion, mixed spices, salt, and pepper.

C. Equal quantities of (i) rice; (ii) tomatoes, peeled and diced very small; (iii) grated onion; and (iv) chopped parsley and dill, all moistened with oil, salt, and pepper.

188   Dulma — Mixed vegetables, stuffed
       Egypt

3–4 white slender eggplants
3–4 brown slender eggplants
3–4 zucchini
3–4 tomatoes
3–4 sweet green peppers
2–3 cups tomato juice
1 tablespoon vinegar
cooking oil
salt and pepper
stuffing (see 187)

Core, seed, and/or empty vegetables. Mix stuffing ingredients and fill vegetables loosely, allowing room for rice to swell. Arrange vegetables in pot, with openings facing up. Sprinkle tomato juice on top. Add vinegar, seasoning, and 1 cup of water to remaining tomato juice, stir, and add to pot to a depth of 2–3 cms. Cook over moderate flame.

The Iraqis also include stuffed leafy vegetables like vine leaves, chard, and cabbage in their dulma.

The Cypriots call their mixed stuffed vegetables *yemista* and include artichoke hearts.

189   Briami — Vegetable casserole
Cyprus

> 3 potatoes, peeled and diced
> 1/2 kg zucchini, peeled and sliced into rounds
> 3 green sweet peppers, seeded and chopped
> 4 tomatoes, peeled and diced
> 2 onions, chopped
> 5–7 garlic cloves, crushed
> 2 tablespoons parsley leaves, chopped
> 1 tablespoon dill or fennel, chopped
> dash of sugar
> olive oil
> salt and pepper

Lightly fry onions until golden, then add peppers and cook for 5 minutes. Grease oven dish and toss in all ingredients. Cover and cook in moderate oven until all vegetables are very tender.

190   Turli— Casserole of mixed vegetables
Egypt

> 1/2 kg beef
> 2–3 potatoes, peeled and diced
> 5–7 pearl onions, peeled
> 1/4 kg okra, see 115
> 1 brown round eggplant, peeled and cubed
> 1/4 kg string beans, halved lengthwise

1 cup peas, shelled

1 teaspoon mint powder

1 hot pepper, chopped very fine

cooking fat

salt and pepper

Cut meat into bite-size cubes and fry until the juice is reabsorbed. Remove from pan and place in casserole dish. Toss all the vegetables—except the hot pepper—into remaining cooking oil and sauté. Strain, add to meat, together with mint powder, hot pepper, and seasoning, and cover with water. Cook over very low flame until vegetables are tender.

In Turkey, this dish is called *turlu*. The ingredients and cooking methods are the same, except that parsley leaves are used instead of mint.

191   Mnazzaleh — Stewed mixed vegetables
      Lebanon, Syria, and Jordan

1/2 cup chickpeas

2 round brown eggplants

3 onions, chopped coarsely

7–10 garlic cloves, sliced diagonally

3–5 tomatoes, peeled and diced

2 tablespoons coriander leaves, chopped

2 tablespoons parsley leaves, chopped

1/2 teaspoon mint powder

pinch of nutmeg or cinnamon

cooking oil

salt and pepper

Soak chickpeas overnight. Drain and set aside.

Peel eggplant, slice, and sprinkle with salt. After about 1 hour, squeeze out moisture, pat dry, and deep fry in sizzling oil. Remove onto absorbent paper.

In the same oil, fry onions until dark, then add tomatoes, garlic, and chickpeas and cook for 20 minutes, or until chickpeas are tender (add more hot water if needed). When ready, add fried eggplant, 1 tablespoon each of parsley and coriander, mint, and nutmeg or cinnamon. Simmer for 10 minutes longer, then remove from flame and allow to cool. Serve warm, topping with remaining parsley and coriander.

Vine Leaves

192 Vine leaves

Vine leaves can be bought fresh, frozen, or already boiled and ready for stuffing. If bought fresh, prepare as follows.

Rinse vine leaves, join the stalks of about 20 together, tie with thread to form a neat bundle, and blanch in salted water for 5 minutes. If frozen or already boiled, rinse to wash away the salt.

To stuff, first cut off the stalks of the vine leaves with a sharp knife, (do not discard them; they can be used to line the bottom of the pot). Carefully pick up each vine leaf and spread out on a smooth surface, shiny side down. Spoon stuffing on the leaf in the direction of veins, arranging it pencil-thin, about 1 cm away from both ends. Fold in the ends, then with tips of thumbs and index fingers, fold in the middle and roll tightly.

193 Waraq dawali — Stuffed vine leaves
Lebanon, Syria, and Jordan

1/2 kg vine leaves
1/2 kg lean lamb, minced
1 to 1 1/2 cups rice
1 kg ripe tomatoes, peeled and diced
bones (preferably with bone marrow)

dash of saffron

dash of mixed spices

cooking fat

salt and pepper

Wash and boil bones in salted water, then place in the bottom of a pot with vine leaf stalk. If bone marrow is used, shake the marrow onto stock first. Mix meat, rice, spices, and seasoning and stuff vine leaves as in 192. Arrange stuffed vine leaves over bones, spooning tomatoes over each layer.

Adjust seasoning of stock, pour over stuffed vine leaves, and cook over moderate flame. When ready, turn over onto serving dish and discard bones and stalks.

194   Wara' 'inab mahshi — Stuffed vine leaves
       Egypt

1/2 kg vine leaves

meat stock

2–3 tablespoons lemon juice

cooking oil

filling A

   1 kg lamb or beef, minced

   2 cups rice

   2 onions, chopped very fine

   salt and pepper

filling B

   2 cups rice

   2–3 carrots, grated

   2–3 onions, grated

   2–3 tomatoes, peeled and diced

   1 cup parsley, chopped very fine

   1 1/2 cups oil

   salt and pepper

Make desired stuffing and stuff vine leaves as in 192. Arrange neatly in pot over stalks, dabbing small pieces of cooking oil among the stuffed layers. Cover with well-seasoned water or stock and cook over moderate flame for 30 minutes. When ready, turn over onto serving dish, discard stalks, and sprinkle with lemon juice.

195　Koopepeya — Stuffed vine leaves
Cyprus

1/2 kg vine leaves
1/2 kg mixture of veal and lamb, minced
1 cup rice
1 tablespoon parsley, chopped very fine
1 onion, chopped very fine
1 tablespoon mint, chopped very fine
2 tablespoons lemon juice
2 cups meat stock
corn oil
salt and pepper
sauce
　　2 eggs
　　2 tablespoons lemon juice
　　1 tablespoon flour
　　1 cup stock
　　2 tablespoons corn oil
　　salt and pepper

Prepare vine leaves as in 192. Fry onion until golden and mix with meat, rice, herbs, seasoning, and oil. Use this mixture to stuff the vine leaves (see 192). Add lemon juice to broth, pour over vine leaves, and cook over moderate flame.

To prepare the sauce, heat corn oil and stir in the flour and cook without browning. Add stock, stirring continually, and allow sauce to thicken. Beat eggs in a bowl until frothy and add lemon juice. Pour hot sauce over egg mixture, beat-

ing constantly, then return to flame and allow eggs to cook
(not boil) for 2 minutes.

Serve stuffed vine leaves and sauce separately.

196   Dolmadakiya — Stuffed vine leaves
        Turkey

        1/2 kg vine leaves
        1/2 kg lamb, minced
        1 cup rice, boiled
        2 onions, chopped finely
        2 tablespoons mint, chopped finely
        1 cup olive oil
        2 tablespoons lemon juice
        2 cups meat stock flavored with coriander seeds
        salt and pepper

Heat about 2 tablespoons olive oil and fry onions until
they wilt. Remove onions, setting aside the oil. Mix together
boiled rice, onions, meat, mint, seasoning, and stuff vine
leaves (see 192).

Pour olive oil in the bottom of the pan, tilt the pan to
coat sides, then tightly pack in the vine leaves. Mix lemon
juice, meat stock, and oil and sprinkle over vine leaves.
Cover and simmer for 30–40 minutes.

Yoghurt

197   Zabadi (Egypt), Laban, or Laban hamed (Lebanon,
        Syria, and Jordan) — yoghurt

        milk
        2 tablespoons yoghurt* for each liter of milk
        or
        1 teaspoon yoghurt for each glass of milk

To prepare home-made yoghurt, warm milk to 37° Celsius (100° Fahrenheit) in summer and 40° Celsius (104° Fahrenheit) in winter—use a thermometer to check temperatures and thus ensure success.

To make a large quantity, stir yoghurt in earthenware or Pyrex container (neither metal or plastic) and pour the warm milk gradually over it, stirring constantly. Cover well and leave in a warm place that will maintain the temperature as long as possible—either a warm oven or covered with a blanket. After about 10 hours, place in refrigerator for one hour before using.

To make yoghurt in individual glasses, stir yoghurt in each glass, add warm milk, and proceed as above.

* The use of yoghurt as a starter depends on whether the ready-made yoghurt is sterilized or not. However, if you are using home-made yoghurt as a starter, it should be used within 3–5 days, otherwise the balance of bacteria in the culture changes, leading to inconsistent results.

198   Cooking yoghurt

1 kg yoghurt
2 egg whites

Beat egg whites until frothy, then stir into yoghurt and pass through sieve into cooking pot. The eggs stabilize the yoghurt and keep it from curdling. Yoghurt should always be cooked uncovered, as condensed steam will spoil it.

199   Laban ummu (Palestine) and Shakriyeh (Lebanon)

1 kg lamb
3–4 cups yoghurt
6–8 pearl onions, peeled and halved
3–5 cardamom seeds, bashed open
bay leaf
2 egg whites
salt and pepper

Cut meat into bite-size pieces. Boil meat, onions, and spices tied in muslin bag in very little water for 20 minutes, or until meat is nearly done. Discard bag, mash onions, add seasoning, and stir in the yoghurt (see 198), and cook for 10 more minutes.

200   Yogurtulu kebap — Kebab with yoghurt
      Turkey

    1 kg lamb
    4–6 slices toast bread
    4–6 tomatoes, peeled and diced
    2 onions, grated
    2 tablespoons lemon juice
    2 cups yoghurt
    1 tampon paprika
    cooking oil
    salt and pepper

Cut lamb into bite-size cubes and marinate in a mixture of onions, lemon juice, and salt for at least 1 hour. Brush off marinade and fry over low flame until tender. Remove and keep warm.

Sauté tomatoes in the same oil, season, and cook until the sauce thickens.

To serve, place the bread in a serving dish, cover with warm tomato sauce, and top with pieces of lamb. Stir the paprika and seasoning into the yoghurt and pour over meat.

Zucchini

201   Zucchini

Zucchini has a very thin fluff which attracts grit. To remove grit, brush under running tap water, rinse in several changes of water, or—better still—peel very thinly.

Zucchini comes in different sizes. The smaller-size ones (10–12 cms long and 3–4 cms in diameter) are mainly used for stuffing. To core zucchini, have at hand some kitchen salt. With a sharp knife, cut off the stem, dip zucchini in the salt, and pierce and core, rotating gently in the palm of your hand. The salt prevents the zucchini from breaking at the opening. Rinse before using.

202 Peynirli kabak — Zucchini, grilled
Turkey

1 kg zucchini

1 cup *beyaz peynir* (feta cheese), crumbled

1 tablespoon hard white cheese, grated

2 tablespoons dill, chopped very fine

3–5 garlic cloves, crushed

2 tablespoons flour

butter

pepper

Parboil zucchini in salted water, drain, and allow to cool. Slice lengthwise and scoop out pulp.

Mix cheeses, flour, dill, and garlic. Fill zucchini and dab with dots of butter. Grill and sprinkle with freshly ground black pepper.

203 Kabak kizartmasi — Zucchini fritters
Turkey

1 kg zucchini

cooking oil

batter

    1 cup flour

    1 teaspoon salt

    1/2 cup beer

Peel and slice zucchini. Mix batter ingredients and
beat until smooth. Dip each slice in batter and shallow fry
in sizzling oil.

204   Kosa mihshiyeh ma' bandura — Stuffed zucchini
       cooked in tomato sauce
       Lebanon

1 kg zucchini
1/2 kg lamb or beef, minced
1/2 cup rice
1 tablespoon parsley, chopped very fine
2 onions, chopped very fine
1–2 tablespoons pine nuts
1 tablespoon mixed spices
sauce
    5–7 garlic cloves, crushed
    2 tomatoes, peeled and diced
    1 teaspoon cinnamon powder
    1 onion, grated
    2 tablespoons tomato paste
    cooking fat
    salt and pepper

Core zucchini (see 201). Mix all ingredients well and
fill zucchini.

To prepare sauce, fry onions until golden, then add
garlic, diced tomatoes, tomato paste dissolved in 1 cup of
water, cinnamon, and seasoning and boil for 10–15 minutes
to thicken sauce. Remove from flame, place stuffed zucchini
in tomato sauce, and cook until both zucchini and stuffing
are well done, about 30 minutes.

205 Kosa mihshiyeh ma' laban — Stuffed zucchini,
cooked in yoghurt
Lebanon

same stuffing ingredients as 204
sauce
    2–3 cups yoghurt
    2 egg whites
    1 teaspoon mint powder
    5–7 garlic cloves, crushed

Prepare zucchini as in 204. To prepare sauce, beat egg
whites until frothy, add to yoghurt with garlic, and blend
well. Pour this mixture through a sieve over cooking zucchini
and cook uncovered for 5–7 minutes. Immediately before
serving, sprinkle with mint powder.

206 Kosa mihshiyeh ma' laban hamed — Stuffed zucchini cooked in yoghurt (1)
Palestine

1 kg zucchini
savory minced beef, 100
2 cups yoghurt
2 egg whites

Core zucchini and fill with savory minced beef. Place in
pot with water to cover and cook over very low flame.
    Beat egg whites and stir into yoghurt. When zucchini
is tender, pour the yoghurt through a sieve over the zucchini
and cook uncovered for 5–7 minutes.
    For a richer dish, lightly fry the zucchini after coring.

207 Kosa mihshiyeh ma' laban hamed — Stuffed zucchini with yoghurt (2)
Palestine

1 kg zucchini

savory minced beef 100
2 cups yoghurt
5–7 garlic cloves, crushed
4–6 toast bread

Core zucchini and fill with savory minced beef. Place in
a pot with just enough water to cover and cook over very low
flame. Mix garlic with yoghurt. Place toast in shallow flat
serving dish. Immediately before serving, heat zucchini,
spoon resulting juice over the bread to soften, then tidily arrange the zucchini over the toast and top with yoghurt. This
dish cannot be warmed, as the combination of hot stuffed
zucchinis with cold yoghurt is essential.

Pastes and Mixed Spices

208   Biber salcasi — Pepper paste
       Turkey

1/2 kg red peppers, hot
1 small chili pepper
dash of sugar
2 tablespoons olive oil
salt

Blend peppers, sugar, and salt with 2–3 cups water in
a food processor, then place in cooking pot over medium
flame and cook until consistency is thick. Stir in the oil and
chill overnight before using.

209   Hrous — Pepper paste
       Tunisia

1 hot red chili pepper
1 teaspoon black pepper powder

1/2 teaspoon cinnamon
1/2 teaspoon caraway seeds
2 onions, chopped very fine
pinch of turmeric
1/2 teaspoon tabil, 213
3 tablespoons olive oil
2 tablespoons salt

Place onions, turmeric, and salt in bowl and allow to rest for two days, when they will become wet and soft. Squeeze to extract moisture.

Remove stems and seeds of chilis and chop coarsely. Soak in boiling water for 30 minutes, then drain and pat dry.

Place all ingredients in a blender and whirl to a smooth thick paste. Place in a jar, top with a thin layer of olive oil, cover, and refrigerate.

210   Muhammarah — Red pepper and walnut dip
Syria

1/2 kg red peppers, hot
1/2 cup walnuts, crushed
2 tablespoons lemon juice
1 tablespoon pomegranate juice
1 teaspoon sugar
dash of cumin
1/2 loaf stale bread
1 tablespoon olive oil.

Roast peppers until blistered all over. Slit open, remove seeds, stem, and skin and set aside.

Boil the pomegranate juice and sugar until thick. Place all ingredients—except the oil—in a food processor or mortar and whirl or pound to reach a creamy blend. Place in jar, sprinkle top with olive oil, and chill overnight.

211   Zhug — Mixed spices
      Yemen

      20 garlic cloves
      5 cardamom pods
      1 teaspoon caraway seeds
      4 peppers, red and hot
      1 cup coriander leaves
      1 teaspoon black pepper
      1 tablespoon salt

Place all ingredients in blender or mortar and whirl or
pound until well blended. Store in jar with tight-fitting lid.

212   Boharat — Mixed spices
      Egypt

A combination of cinnamon, cloves, nutmeg, cumin, coriander, and pepper all crushed together in powder form.
Paprika is added to give the mixture a brown tinge.

213   Tabil — Mixed spices
      Tunisia

A combination of coriander, caraway, fennel, aniseed,
cumin tumeric, garlic, and pepper crushed in powder form.

214   Harissa — Hot chili paste
      Tunisia

      3 tablespoons hot chili
      3 tablespoons mild chili
      1 teaspoon coriander
      1 teaspoon caraway
      3–5 garlic cloves
      1 red hot pepper
      olive oil
      salt

Remove stems and seeds of chilis and pepper and chop coarsely. Soak in boiling water for 30 minutes, then drain and squeeze dry.

Place all ingredients in blender with enough oil to form a thick paste. Store in a jar, top with a thin layer of oil, cover, and refrigerate

Recipes Listed by Name

129

Recipes Listed by Country

Note: Numbers refer to recipes.

Cyprus

Iran

Turkey

All Arab Countries

Lebanon, Syria, and Jordan

Gulf States

Egypt

Iraq

Jordan

Index

141

From the couscous of North Africa to the kebab of Iraq, from the stuffed vine leaves of the Levant to the spices of the Arabian Peninsula, this new companion volume to *Egyptian Cooking: A Practical Guide* by the same author reveals the colorful and tasty gamut of cuisines of the Middle East. Color photographs accompany clear, easy-to-follow recipes for over 200 delicious mezze, breakfast, and main course dishes from all over the Arab world, as well as Iran, Turkey, and Cyprus.

Samia Abdennour came to Egypt from Palestine in 1947. She is married and has four children.

Cover photographs by Ola Seif

ISBN 977-424-401-X

9 789774 244018

90000

 The American University in Cairo Press

106   Meat patties, fried
146   Bread salad

Lebanon

8   Roasted and puréed eggplant with pomegranate juice
9   Roasted eggplant with yoghurt
11   Kibbeh patties
32   Baked eggs in yoghurt
50   Stuffed cabbage, meatless
53   Chicken cooked with lemon
56   Stuffed chicken, boiled and fried
58   Stuffed chicken, roasted
65   Couscous cooked with chicken
83   Fried liver
104   Meatballs, baked
105   Meat patties, fried
125   Turnovers with cheese filling
126   Turnovers with meat filling
134   Rice and chicken pilaf
145   Beetroot salad
199   Lamb cooked in yoghurt
204/5   Stuffed zucchini cooked in tomato sauce

Palestine

12   Raw liver
14   Pastry with oregano spread
27   Fried eggs with white cheese
28   Fried eggs with garlic
42   Stuffed artichokes
44   Stewed artichokes
51   Stuffed cabbage
55   Chicken roasted with sumac
67   Creamy eggplant
74   Eggplant, stuffed
76   Fish baked in tahina sauce
103   Meat patties, fried
120/1   Pastry with meat filling
127   Pastry filled with meat and cooked in yoghurt
141   Rice cooked with spinach
146   Bread salad
168   Sheep's head soup

Index

141